*Advance Praise for*

# Peace, Justice, and the Poetic Mind

This latest in a series of books documenting conversations between Daisaku Ikeda, president of Soka Gakkai International, and leading global citizens features Dr. Stuart Rees, peace activist and professor emeritus of the University of Sydney. Topics for the twelve dialogues featured in this text range from the family histories and upbringings of both speakers to the individual nuances of their shared vision for a peace-, justice-, and joy-filled future for the world community. The authors' sensitive and compassionate insights on the current condition of humanity are rendered even more powerful by frequent citations of poetry. While there is much in this book to engage the intellect, the numerous quoted verses speak to a deeper realm of the reader's psyche.

—Isabel Nunez, Professor and Chair of the Department of Educational Studies, Purdue University Fort Wayne

In this dialogue, Daisaku Ikeda and Stuart Rees take us on a journey that is rich in insights and delightful in its story telling. As they seamlessly traverse the varied and fertile ground of poetry, spirituality, ethics and identity, we encounter the passion and wisdom of two men whose engagement with the human predicament has never wavered. It is engagement born from a firm grasp of the horrors of war and the enormity of the nuclear peril. But it is also engagement born of the conviction that human effort can make a difference. *Peace, Justice, and the Poetic Mind* offers us a compelling diagnosis of our ills. More than that, it points to the nonviolent pathway that leads to a just peace, and offers the pilgrim of peace much needed encouragement and inspiration.

—Joseph Camilleri, OAM, Emeritus Professor of International Relations, La Trobe University, Melbourne

# Peace, Justice, and the Poetic Mind

# Peace, Justice, and the Poetic Mind

Conversations on the Path of Nonviolence

STUART REES

DAISAKU IKEDA

Dialogue Path Press
Cambridge, Massachusetts
2018

Published by Dialogue Path Press
Ikeda Center for Peace, Learning, and Dialogue
396 Harvard Street
Cambridge, Massachusetts 02138

Cover design by Gopa & Ted2, Inc.
Interior design by Gopa & Ted2, Inc., and Eric Edstam

ISBN: 978-1-88917-19-3

Library of Congress Cataloging-in-Publication Data

Names: Rees, Stuart, 1939- author. | Ikeda, Daisaku, author.
Title: Peace, justice, and the poetic mind : conversations on the path of
nonviolence / Stuart Rees, Daisaku Ikeda.
Description: Cambridge, Massachusetts : Dialogue Path Press, [2018]
Includes bibliographical references and index.
Identifiers: LCCN 2018018720 | ISBN 9781887917193 (pbk.: alk. paper)
Subjects: LCSH: Nonviolence. | Peace. | Social justice.
Classification: LCC HM1281 .R436 2018 | DDC 303.6/1—dc23
LC record available at https://lccn.loc.gov/2018018720

10 9 8 7 6 5 4 3 2 1

# About Dialogue Path Press

Dialogue Path Press is the publishing arm of the Ikeda Center for Peace, Learning, and Dialogue, and is dedicated to publishing titles that foster cross-cultural dialogue and greater human flourishing. Books published by the Center (including those produced in collaboration with other publishers before the establishment of Dialogue Path Press) have been used in more than 900 college and university courses. Previous titles are:

*Shaping a New Society: Conversations on Economics, Education, and Peace* (2017)

*Knowing Our Worth: Conversations on Energy and Sustainability* (2016)

*Our World To Make: Hinduism, Buddhism, and the Rise of Global Civil Society* (2015)

*Living As Learning: John Dewey in the 21st Century* (2014)

*The Art of True Relations: Conversations on the Poetic Heart of Human Possibility* (2014)

*America Will Be!: Conversations on Hope, Freedom, and Democracy* (2013)

*The Inner Philosopher: Conversations on Philosophy's Transformative Power* (2012)

*Into Full Flower: Making Peace Cultures Happen* (2010)

*Creating Waldens: An East-West Conversation on the American Renaissance* (2009)

# About the Ikeda Center

The Ikeda Center for Peace, Learning, and Dialogue was founded by Buddhist philosopher, educator, and peacebuilder Daisaku Ikeda in 1993. Located in Cambridge, Massachusetts, its mission is to establish a shared global ethic across cultures and religions—

an ethic based on respect for the absolute sanctity of life itself, a firm belief in the human potential for good and for transforming the world, and a clear recognition of the interdependence of all life. Ikeda Center programs include the development of multi-author books on topics in peace, learning, and dialogue; a fellows program to advance research on a humanistic form of learning called value-creating education; an annual Ikeda Forum for Intercultural Dialogue; and "Dialogue Nights" for college students and young professionals. The Center was initially called the Boston Research Center for the 21st Century and became the Ikeda Center in 2009.

For more information, visit the Ikeda Center website: www.ikedacenter.org

# Table of Contents

Stuart Rees and Daisaku Ikeda

# Preface

What are the challenges that we need to undertake in the twenty-first century?

It is time we rethink the concept of peace and discard the conventional concept expressed in the ancient Roman proverb, "If you want peace, prepare for war." Instead, we must seek to establish the kind of civilization that chooses nonviolence and denounces war if we are to realize the peaceful coexistence of all.

Countless human lives were sacrificed in the twentieth century in the name of ideological and nationalistic causes. We must no longer tolerate the "justice in name only" that allows the use of any means to achieve an end and capitalizes on human lives. We must instead strive to build a solidarity of people's justice that serves to protect the dignity of all human beings.

Dr. Stuart Rees, who was active as Sydney Peace Foundation director, is a man who has always stood at the forefront to pave the uncharted path toward this goal. I first met him in May 1999[1] amid the brilliance of fresh green leaves. Many teens, their faces young and eager, gathered to welcome him to Tokyo.

With his quick wit, he filled the hall with smiles and laughter. But what left an indelible impression on me was the earnestness with which he reminded the young audience of their shared responsibility to add color to the peaceful vision of an ideal world where all people, regardless of their social status, can fully manifest their creative potential.

Every person is endowed with shining dignity, limitless potential for creativity, and a unique purpose in life only he or she can fulfill. Dr. Rees referred to this as the "promise of biography." He became convinced of his own mission while in the United Kingdom, his birthplace, and Canada, where he toiled as a social worker in his youth, impassioned and driven by lofty ideals.

As young Rees watched people with underprivileged backgrounds living in difficult conditions, their voices unheard, he determined to sympathize with their suffering, lend an ear to their needs, and continue offering all the help he could. Dr. Rees firmly believed that, no matter how hopeless a situation may seem, as long as one is given a chance and a sense of assurance, every person is capable of embarking on a new life.

As our society faces serious crises, it has become clearer that ordinary people must take the initiative to change its course. For a nation to undergo successful post-conflict recovery and reconstruction, it becomes essential to empower individuals at the local level and help them develop their inner strengths. Dr. Rees's conviction is grounded in his priceless experience as a social worker struggling for the sake of the vulnerable.

At a time when it was rare to see universities around the world offer courses in peace studies, it was Dr. Rees who, in his capacity as a professor, fought to realize this in response to students' strong wishes. He founded the Centre for Peace and Conflict Studies at the University of Sydney as a proud example of an institution dedicated to students' needs.

As the founder of Soka University, which first and foremost places importance on our students, I can deeply relate to Dr. Rees's decision to stand up for the students and never retreat in the face of obstacles.

The central theme woven throughout our dialogue is "peace with justice"—a topic he has continued to pursue since he was inaugurated as the first director of the Centre for Peace and Conflict Studies. His unchanging belief (see page four) is that

> peace is not the mere absence of war. Even though a situation may look peaceful on the surface, as long as there are people who suffer from injustice, including poverty and lack of opportunities, that situation is not worthy of the name of peace in its true sense.

I found that Dr. Rees's concept of peace deeply resonates with the conviction of my mentor, Josei Toda, second Soka Gakkai president. Toda courageously stood up to realize the happiness of all people, striving to "eliminate human misery from the face of this earth." He did so during the Cold War era, which was dominated by the belief that peace and security could be founded on a "balance of terror," or, in other words, mutual terror based on symmetrical capabilities of mass destruction.

Based on this common ground, we exchanged our views on a wide range of issues, from abolition of nuclear weapons and the processes of conflict resolution to human rights, poverty, human dignity, and social justice. As a means to dispel the deep darkness that torments our world today, we concurred on the importance of humanistic education that fosters empathy in people, a willingness to share in the suffering of others. We also felt the strong need to revive the poetic spirit that has the power to awaken inherent goodness in people and instill the courage to confront social evil.

At the time of our first encounter, as Dr. Rees presented me with a book he authored, we both agreed that words can become weapons of peace. And that while in times of war, weapons are produced for murder, what is needed now are weapons of peace, by which militarism can be quashed. I believe that while the potential power of one book may seem small, it can actually serve as an important impetus for moving the age in the direction of peace.

This book is a collection of my exchanges on the quest for peace and the way for the realization of social justice with Dr. Rees, whom I deeply respect. It is a book driven by our mutual conviction in the immense power of one book to bring about change.

My sincere hope is that this book will offer insights to young people who shoulder the future and serve as a catalyst to transform the coming era.

*Daisaku Ikeda*
*Tokyo, Japan*

# Preface

A commitment to Buddhism through art, music, poetry, photography, and other art forms has been a significant feature of Daisaku Ikeda's life and leadership. Such a multidimensional way of thinking and living has contributed not only to personal fulfillment but, more important, has encouraged millions of others to engage in activities that enhance everyone's sense of freedom and fulfillment.

In the following twelve conversations between Dr. Ikeda and myself, we refer to such a way of "thinking and living" as the philosophy of peace and the poetic mind. Before sketching the book's contents, I'll make two simple points about the links between peace and poetry.

First, if peace only means a ceasefire in a war or an end to violence in domestic disputes, it is unlikely to have much lasting effect on human rights and on the quality of life of the people involved. But if peace negotiators used their imagination, they could focus on peace with justice, not simply peace. That is a crucial distinction. Striving for peace with justice depends, among other things, on exploring context, country and culture, individual needs and aspirations, and an appreciation of nonviolence.

That brings me to my second point—the value of poetry. In

common with other art forms, poetry strives to convey meaning
that enables readers and listeners to realize ideas and possibilities
that they may have never previously imagined. The poetic mind
cannot tell people what to do but can excite and motivate. The
poetic mind cannot claim to have answers, but thinking poetically
begins to realize human potential because it depends on humor
and insight plus a willingness to laugh at oneself and to ponder
life's wonders, cruelties, and absurdities. Such a way of thinking
and writing brings us, inevitably, to peace with justice.

We start our dialogue with an exchange about the courage
needed to take a stand on issues of war and peace, on questions
about justice and human rights. In this respect, we follow that
wonderful challenge made by the late Stéphane Hessel, French
freedom fighter, concentration camp survivor, diplomat, and co-
architect, along with Eleanor Roosevelt, of the Universal Declaration of Human Rights. At the age of ninety-three, Hessel wrote
the bestselling book *Time for Outrage!*[1] He insisted that to express
outrage about injustice was a crucial life force and the means of
staying in touch with one's humanity. The alternative, he said, was
indifference.

Our dialogue stays in touch with humanity by opposing violence of all kinds, in particular by advocating the creation of a
world without nuclear weapons. President Ikeda's annual peace
messages have appealed for the creation of an international
nuclear disarmament agency. We discuss ways to respond to his
appeal as a national and international priority for any individuals
or groups concerned with promoting peace with justice.

Our dialogue about the philosophy, language, and practice of
nonviolence refers not only to the cultural heritage of Buddhism
but also to a respect for views derived from all religions and from
citizens with no religious beliefs. Such understanding and tolerance is the core of that humanist orientation of peace linked to
poetry.

The philosophy and practice of nonviolence are expressed not merely through the spoken or written word. They can be seen in the way we care for children, the mentally ill, the homeless, the frail elderly, asylum seekers, and refugees. In Mahatma Gandhi's terms, nonviolence is a "law for life." It is also expressed in the way we dress, the manner of decorating our homes, the music we enjoy, the poetry we read, and the hospitality we offer to others.

Protecting and preserving a precious natural environment is another feature of nonviolence. Such a goal could be a political priority for all the world's peoples. Indifference to environmental destruction, or to the possession of nuclear weapons, would be a reason for protest.

A common theme in our dialogue concerns the need to respect the dignity of all human beings and all living things. Such a goal is shown in all thirty clauses of the Universal Declaration of Human Rights and is why we place great faith in "education to nurture a culture of human rights."

All these deliberations lead to views about individual peace of mind and to perspectives on education, on the conduct of business, and on the crafting of social and foreign policies. Such views and perspectives depend on the dominance of altruism over egoism, which is another way of describing the philosophy of peace and the poetic mind.

*Stuart Rees*
*Hyams Beach, New South Wales, Australia*

CONVERSATION ONE

# Peace Is Not Only the Absence of War

REES: I would like to send my most sincere condolences to those who have lost loved ones in the Great East Japan Earthquake and the subsequent catastrophic tsunami (March 2011).[1] Friends of the Soka Gakkai International from the Sydney Peace Foundation offer our expressions of solidarity with all our Japanese colleagues and friends at this tragic and demanding time.

I am reminded of your constant emphasis on the interdependence of all peoples and all living things. In this respect, the awful disaster could be a means to enable all peoples to forget their differences and achieve a sense of common cause for those whose luck may have run out, at least for the time being. In that spirit and in a spirit of solidarity, I send my sincere condolences and personal good wishes to all in the worst-hit areas of your country and across Japan.

IKEDA: Thank you for your warm words of friendship and encouragement. Relief and recovery activities are still being conducted vigorously. SGI members have been doing everything we can to care for the victims by offering counsel and encouragement as well as organizing relief efforts. We are drawing great strength and inspiration from the prayers and support of you and other friends around the world.

Buddhism teaches the principle of changing poison into medicine, which refers to the human potential to emerge strengthened from any trial or adversity when we challenge our circumstances without succumbing to defeat. We can transform difficulty into a source of immense strength and the driving force to create a better life and better society. Moreover, Buddhism maintains that this transformative capacity clearly exists within every human being. In any event, we are fully committed to advance the revival and rebuilding of Japan to serve as a great light of hope for the world.

## EVERYBODY DESERVES PEACE

IKEDA: Humanity is currently confronted by a number of global challenges, including environmental destruction, poverty, a food-supply crisis, terrorism, war and conflict, as well as massive natural disasters like the earthquake and tsunami here in Japan. In order to get through this time of crisis, we need to find a path that takes us to a global society of peace and creative coexistence. Concurrently, we must work to solve these various issues step by step in order to establish "peace with justice."

One of the people who has been working in a wide range of areas at the forefront of this challenge is you, Professor Rees. As an engaged peace scholar, rather than confine yourself to research in your area of study, you have spared no effort to address the plight of people who suffer amid appalling social conditions. Many people are grateful for your unflagging service to others, for you are always there for the suffering, listening to them as you strive to solve their problems. Each and every humanitarian contribution you have made throughout the world—in countries such as the United Kingdom, Canada, the United States, India, and Sri Lanka—is precious. Moreover, you have been strenuous in nurturing an awareness of peace among young people who will shoulder responsibility for the next generation.

I find the opportunity to engage in a dialogue with you to be profoundly meaningful, for you are as much a champion of peace and humanity as you are a poet of conviction and passion.

REES: The pleasure is mine. I have read many of your writings, President Ikeda, and have met you a number of times. Through our meetings, I have felt that you have a rare talent to overcome cultural boundaries and obstacles through dialogue.

It is my unchangeable belief that even though dialogue is sometimes accompanied by seemingly insurmountable difficulties and obstacles, any other path must end in failure and resignation. For that reason, I would like to express my sincere respect for your efforts to activate all the constructive values that dialogue has as you sought to build bridges of friendship and trust in a divided world ever since the time of the Cold War.

In addition, I have been impressed by the vision that you have shown through your annual peace proposals[2] and your lectures at universities around the world, and by how you have been sounding an alarm bell to modern civilization, which often loses sight of humanity. The words and philosophy that you use when you address global issues express a new humanism, and that is what the world continually yearns for.

IKEDA: I am humbled by your praise.

REES: In your 2009 proposal,[3] published in the wake of the once-in-a-century financial meltdown, you pointed out that the latent cause of the breakdown of the financial market was the greed of people in power and their lack of care for others, which brought poverty and unemployment to many people. Referring also to the fact that the people described as the "bottom billion" suffer from starvation and malnutrition due to rising grain prices, you warned of an urgent need for international cooperation in order to secure the stable supply of food, which is essential to sustain human life and protect human dignity. You then addressed the issue of nuclear weapons, which threaten humankind's right to live, stressing that we should move away from policies that try to secure the safety of one's own country only and instead establish as a global norm the principle of never seeking one's own peace and safety at the expense of the fear and unhappiness of others.

All of these are important points, and the direction for transforming the era indicated in your proposal is consistent with our principle, "peace with justice," which is our aim at the Sydney Peace Foundation. "Peace with justice" is a goal both enduring and universal in value and should be shared by all human beings.

Peace is not the mere absence of war. Even though a situation may look peaceful on the surface, as long as there are people who suffer from injustice, including poverty and lack of opportunities, that situation is not worthy of the name of peace in its true sense. I might add that, although peace is a worthy goal, peace with justice will be more lasting and more universally beneficial; and that's a goal for people in all walks of life.

Through this dialogue, I hope we can dig deeply into this theme.

IKEDA: I agree. It is a subject to which I have long devoted much thought as well. This is because it was the fervent wish of my mentor, Josei Toda, the second Soka Gakkai president, to eliminate the word "misery" from the human lexicon. In 1957, the year before he passed away, President Toda said that it was his desire that the word "misery" would no longer have to be used when describing the world, any country, or any individual. He urged us youth to stand up and take action to bring about a peaceful society. One of the key reasons I have engaged in dialogue with numerous individuals around the world and issued proposals and delivered university lectures has been to fulfill this pledge I made with my mentor.

As you have said, however much we may call for peace, if we close our eyes to the plight of those actually suffering, peace will be nothing more than a pipe dream. Instead, we should focus our attention on the dignity and happiness of each individual and make tangible progress one step at a time toward a world where everybody can enjoy genuine peace and where justice in its true sense may be achieved.

Isn't this a challenge that we who live in the twenty-first century should be addressing?

REES: I totally agree. The future of humankind totally depends on whether we succeed in this endeavor.

IKEDA: In addition, it is my hope to discuss in this dialogue ways to strengthen the bonds of friendship and broaden the conduits of exchange between Australia and Japan.

President Toda proposed a concept of global citizenship, explaining that we need to build a society in which no peoples are sacrificed and where the dignity of every life can be respected equally. My mentor was thinking of Australia in particular, given its immense potential as a nation endowed with great ethnic and cultural diversity.

The University of Sydney, where you taught for many years, has been a fount of wisdom and activity helping to sustain Australia's progress and development—like an electric dynamo, if you will. It enjoys an illustrious tradition not only as the oldest, but also as one of the foremost seats of higher learning in Australia. Hosting researchers from more than eighty countries and more than 10,000 foreign exchange students, the University of Sydney is renowned as a model university—a truly international university linked to every part of the world.

It has already been more than ten years since I had the pleasure of attending a special graduation ceremony held in Singapore for overseas students graduating from your university (in November 2000). My memories of that occasion remain vivid to this day. Professor Dame Leonie Kramer was the chancellor at that time, and each time she presented a student with a diploma, she spoke warmly to that student like an affectionate mother, congratulating each student on his or her new departure setting foot into adult society. You were also present, applauding and watching over the students like a caring father. It was a beautiful scene to behold, just like a magnificent painting, really bringing home to me the spirit of your university, which treasures its students above all else.

REES: I am happy to hear that. We started holding graduation ceremonies outside Australia with the intention of letting family and friends of overseas students join the celebration upon their graduation. There are many students from Asian countries in particular. Therefore, in addition to Singapore, we also conduct ceremonies in Hong Kong every year.

It was an honor for the University to award the honorary Doctor of Letters to you at the graduation ceremony in Singapore for your continuous work for peace. When you delivered your acceptance speech, you created an atmosphere as if you were conducting one-on-one dialogue with the students. I remember being impressed with the warm and friendly manner in which you delivered your speech.

It is my belief that the following two elements are necessary if dialogue is to successfully connect people's hearts. The first is the desire to truly understand the "life biography" of the person with whom you are in dialogue, and the second is humor and compassion.

I am particularly attracted to your robust sense of humor, which manifests the sense of trust toward humanity that is essential for living through the present age. I have never forgotten that strong feeling when I first met you in Tokyo in May 1999. On that occasion, at a meeting where many young people gathered, you talked about the importance of improving themselves while they were young, as well as the importance of friendship and being filial to their parents. There was no preaching tone, and your message was truly from the heart. I was moved to see the audience's true feelings in response to a speech interspersed with humor.

IKEDA: Thank you very much. That was a gathering of Soka Gakkai elementary, junior, and senior high school students, and it was carried out on Children's Day (May 5), a national holiday in Japan. I recall that you instantly grabbed the hearts of the young people in your speech as well, causing them to break out in broad smiles. You clearly presented your vision toward peace. I have always believed that we should not treat boys and girls in a patronizing manner. I have engaged youth with my entire being in hopes of sowing the seeds of hope, courage, and triumph in the rich earth of their young lives.

The Soka Gakkai thus designates May 5 "Successors Day," a day to reaffirm the importance of fostering the next generation of leaders. The state of a society's health is determined by the extent to which adults cherish the young generation—the treasure of our future—and by the passion with which we devote ourselves to their happiness.

In the words of the great English poet John Milton, "The childhood shews the man, As morning shews the day."[4] If a lifetime should be likened to a single day, then it is vital to shine the proper kind of light and sow the proper kind of seed in the morning of a child's life. This is why I would like to begin this dialogue by learning about your childhdood. Where were you born?

## CHARLES DICKENS

REES: I was born in a village about 12 miles from Portsmouth in southern England on October 9, 1939, along with my twin brother, a few weeks after World War II started. Just before I was born, we moved so that my father could commute easily to Portsmouth, where the naval base was located—home port for the United Kingdom fleet.

During the war, my father was seldom at home, and my mother prepared us for life in the countryside. We were surrounded by fields, woods, brooks, and ponds. She used to take us—myself and my brother—to teach us the names and characteristics of trees, wildflowers and edible nuts, wild berries, and mushrooms.

IKEDA: She was a wise mother, wasn't she? You must have learned about the wonder and greatness of life and nurtured a rich poetic mind through your exposure to nature. I sense your mother's deep love and wisdom.

Speaking of Portsmouth, this is also where the great writer Charles Dickens was born. Among the books recommended by President Toda for the development of young people was Dickens's *A Tale of Two Cities*—a masterpiece set in Paris and London at the time of the French Revolution. I have fond memories of this work and have enjoyed reading it many times.

Not only was I impressed by Dickens's works, I also empathized strongly with the way he lived as a young boy. The eldest son among numerous siblings, he led a life of poverty and had to work in a factory from the age of twelve. The family lived in London at the time, but his father, who had repeatedly foundered financially, was at one time sent to prison for failing to repay a loan.

The last despairing words Dickens's father said to him were to the effect that the sun had set upon him forever. "I really believed at the time . . . that [these words] had broken my heart," Dickens stated.[5]

But the young Dickens was never defeated in any sense of the word. Whenever he found time, he would go to the British Museum and read voraciously, continuing his studies even though he could not attend school as he wished. Later, having gone through a variety of jobs, he became a newspaper reporter and eventually achieved great success as a novelist. He is often described as a writer who excelled in depicting the subtleties of the mind. Could this be attributed largely to the fact that he had to endure a succession of ordeals from boyhood and prevailed over them through tenacious struggle?

REES: I agree with what you say. The works of Dickens are widely read even today by many people in the United Kingdom. His birthplace on the outskirts of Portsmouth is well preserved, and it is also a tourist spot.

## EFFECTS OF WAR

IKEDA: Portsmouth has a sister-city agreement with Maizuru City in Kyoto, Japan. Maizuru shares a similar history with Portsmouth as a harbor city that once prospered as a naval port. When the sister-city agreement was signed in May 1998, Portsmouth representatives visited the World Brick Museum in Maizuru and presented a brick from Dickens's birthplace. I have close friends in both Maizuru and Portsmouth.

Another reason I empathize with Dickens's childhood is because it parallels my own experience when my father was ill and bedridden for nearly five years. My father was stricken with rheumatism when I was in the second grade. Our family's once prosperous *nori* (edible seaweed) processing business had to be scaled back considerably. We suffered financial hardship from that time onward.

In those days, we lived in a large, two-story house on the shore of Tokyo Bay. We had a sizeable garden in which stood pomegranate and tall cherry trees. There was also a pond where migratory birds would briefly rest their wings before moving on.

I was very fond of that house with its many places to play. However, when my father started to recover, my eldest brother, the mainstay of our family, was sent off to war, and in the end we had to give up the house. After that, my second eldest brother and then my third eldest brother were drafted into military service. Our life became even harder.

I wanted to make myself useful, no matter how modest my contribution. So I would get up early in the morning to help with preparing *nori* and then start my newspaper route. I went to school, and when I came home I would help with the family business once again and after that go out to deliver the evening papers. Those days were quite tough on me because my constitution was poor. Nevertheless, I seriously wanted to be of assistance to my mother, who was supporting our family all by herself.

A better quality of seaweed can be produced in colder water, so the coldest month of January was our busiest period. The sea before dawn felt freezing cold. With frozen hands, I would ride my bike to the newspaper distribution center to prepare for my paper route.

I kept this up for nearly three years, as a result of which my legs became well conditioned. I believe I then laid the foundation for my physical strength, which later enabled me to travel the length and breadth of Japan and all over the world.

One thing that I will never forget from those days is the expression of disbelief and anxiety on people's faces when I handed them the newspaper telling of Japan's attack on Pearl Harbor, signaling the outbreak of war between Japan and the United States. Before long, my fourth eldest brother, who was immediately above me, was also conscripted.

REES: You had a tremendous struggle, didn't you? I can imagine your feelings while your father was ill in bed. This is because my own father was also badly injured, in a naval battle somewhere off the coast of Java, Indonesia. He survived, and after returning home he had to spend years having operations and convalescing. During that time, we visited him in a hospital many times. We saw many young men there who had suffered horrific war injuries.

Despite all this, I never heard my father complain, and he refused to be registered as disabled. He had always loved music and playing the piano. But he lost the use of both hands from the injury he suffered during the war, and it became impossible for him to play the piano for the rest of his life. However, he would sing in choirs with a wonderful tenor voice and probably inspired others in this way. I greatly admired my father.

IKEDA: I understand that your father's injury was the result of a torpedo attack by the Imperial Japanese Navy. What outrageous, inhuman acts Japan perpetrated time and time again during the war! So many people were injured and caused to suffer, including your father. As a Japanese, I offer my heartfelt apologies. As a Buddhist, I have offered prayers for your late mother and father.

The Soka Gakkai's first and second presidents, Tsunesaburo Makiguchi and Josei Toda, firmly opposed Japan's militarism, which endorsed acts of aggression and barbarity. While they were eventually imprisoned for their stand, they refused to compromise their convictions to the very end. The extant records of President Makiguchi's interrogation in prison show that he conceded nothing to the authorities and steadfastly remonstrated against the fallacy of militarism without retreating a single step.

In no way could the invasion and occupation of China and other

Asian countries be described as a "holy war," which was how Japanese militarists sought to justify it. Rather, it was a fundamentally flawed attempt at thought control by the state, which resulted in total madness.

President Makiguchi died in prison, nursing to the very end the hope for a ceaseless procession of successors to advance peace and happiness for all humanity. He died on November 18, 1944, at age seventy-three.

President Toda, who was eventually released from prison, went on to realize his late mentor's cherished desire. After the war, he poured all his energies into constructing a mighty movement for peace in which enlightened citizens from every walk of life would never allow Japan to repeat the mistakes that led to war. He also devoted himself to fostering young people who would shoulder this responsibility for generations to come.

Up until this day, I have continued to strive for the sake of world peace, embracing the spirit of the first two presidents as my own. Their struggle is the eternal launching point for the SGI's peace movement.

REES: The struggle by the Soka Gakkai's three successive presidents for the sake of peace and humanity is truly noble. Through exchange with Soka University, which you founded, and through research cooperation with the Toda Institute for Global Peace and Policy Research and other projects, I have come to know that the spirit of the first two presidents has been handed down to the present day and continues to generate hope. I am deeply impressed by this.

I have previously written the following (in 2000) with such thoughts in mind:

> The post-war development of Japan should not be recognized only by the economic and technological success of her big industries. Like the Japanese people, the people

of the world should express their gratitude to Makiguchi, Toda and Ikeda, who are leaders of the nonviolent movement in Japan. The 55th anniversary of the cessation of hostilities should be a day for celebrating the lives and achievements of these leaders of nonviolence in Japan.[6]

IKEDA: I am grateful to you for accurately evaluating the achievements of my two mentors. I wish to dedicate your words to them.

President Makiguchi often urged young people that it was more important to be the lone lion than one of a thousand sheep. Your father, who stoutly lived with conviction, undefeated by difficulty, was a lion.

What did you learn from your father that continues to occupy a special place in your heart to this day?

REES: As a boy from a poor family, he left school early to join the navy. He didn't graduate from high school, but nevertheless he was very wise and had a sound philosophy of life. This was because he gained a priceless education from his life at sea and onboard ships. He gained a unique wisdom from such experiences.

The lesson I learned from my father is that we should take life seriously but not take ourselves too seriously. He often said that if you started on a project, you should finish it despite the obstacles in your way. I believe that this applies to everything in life, from long distance running to difficult schoolwork—such as mathematics or Latin—to overcoming opposition in campaigns for social justice.

His concern for others and his gratefulness for small mercies were also unforgettable lessons. He never complained about his injuries or the years of hospital treatment that hindered his reentry into the work force. He was always cheerful, optimistic, and thankful that he survived. At the same time, he felt keenly the injustice that many of his young friends lost their lives.

IKEDA: It sounds like he was a wonderful father. You took his spirit to heart and carried it forward, taking action for the sake of world peace to this day. This is a great victory in the drama of life, one achieved by father and son through the bonds that unite them.

On hearing your story, I am reminded of the time I was invited to visit the historian Arnold J. Toynbee at his home in London. In the room next to the drawing room where we were conducting our dialogue, there was a mantelpiece over the fireplace on which stood about twenty small frames with photographs of young men. When I gazed at them, he said quietly, "Friends from my days at Oxford University: They were all killed in action in World War I."

When young men were being sent off to the war one after another, Dr. Toynbee had to be hospitalized due to an illness he had contracted before the war. His fellow students were in their late twenties. They were at the precious age when they were about to fulfill important roles on the biggest stage of their lives, but instead, these "best and brightest" young people lost their lives in the war.

With tears in his eyes, he told me, "The older you become, the more poignantly you remember those men...sacrificed to war." He recalled that he could never forget the faces of women who wept bitterly as they looked at a notice board announcing those killed in action during the war. In his *Experiences*, he wrote:

> I can see those two poor women's faces as clearly today in my mind's eye as, on that day, I saw them in the life. While I still have life and strength, I must work for the abolition of the wicked institution that was the cause of that terrible sorrow.[7]

I lost my beloved eldest brother, Kiichi, to the war. The war eventually ended in 1945, and my other brothers returned home in a state of total despair and exhaustion, but for a long time we received no news of Kiichi. One day in May 1947, after nearly two years, we received official notification that he had died in Burma (present-day Myanmar).

Although fraught with concern, my mother had been wishing every day for his safe return, and the sight of her back shuddering with grief as she cried is burned indelibly into my mind. It was three months afterward that I met President Toda and began to strive for world peace and the happiness of humanity.

What recollections do you have of the wartime years?

REES: Though I was very young, memories of air raids remain vivid. Portsmouth was a naval base of considerable military importance. The city was heavily bombed by the German air force, and those attacks reached the areas around Portsmouth. I recall a large anti-aircraft gun site in our small garden, bomb craters in nearby fields. During bombing raids, we slept in an air-raid shelter among vegetables grown in the garden. I also remember watching my mother preparing food for allied troops whose tanks sat outside our home in readiness for the 1944 invasion of Normandy.

My commitment to peace did not emerge directly from these childhood experiences or the fact that my father was seriously injured in the war, but they undoubtedly influenced my deep dislike of violence.

IKEDA: Air raids are truly terrifying. Not only was our family's house razed, but our relatives also lost their homes in such raids.

We were forced to sell our house because of my father's protracted illness and move into a house nearby. However, the authorities ordered that house to be demolished, their reason being that firebreaks had to be built because the bombing of Tokyo was intensifying.

We were forced to evacuate. We added a wing to a house

belonging to one of our relatives and decided to live there. As soon as we had moved in all the furniture, on the night before our new life was to begin, there was an air raid. Our new home and our relative's house received a direct hit and burned to the ground.

On another day, there was an intense air raid, with incendiary bombs falling from the skies one after the other; everywhere we looked was engulfed in a sea of fire, and flames burned the night sky red. That sight I remember vividly to this day, along with the terror I felt as I fled, holding my younger brother's hand. In addition, the image of an old couple fleeing in terror during an aerial bombardment in the middle of the night is permanently engraved in my mind.

You mentioned that your wartime experiences influenced your deep dislike of violence. I, too, am certain that the memories impressed on my soul from my experiences at the time will never dim. Their influence transcends the realms of theory or politics.

Having inherited the banner of peace and humanism from President Makiguchi and President Toda, I have striven onward for half a century during which I have had to forge through never-ending difficulties and ordeals, as if proceeding along a series of precipitous, rugged mountain ridges. From the beginning, I have been prepared for heartless criticism and slander.

When I visited the Soviet Union and China during the Cold War, I received an endless stream of threatening letters and telephone calls. But I was determined that I could not and would not compromise in the slightest.

President Makiguchi insisted that, in order to accomplish great good for ourselves, for others, and for society as a whole, we must not be distracted by criticism or submit to blind obedience. He wrote:

The root cause of evil in modern times lies in people's misconceptions about not doing good. They mistake not doing good as being the same as doing good, and think not doing good is different from evil; and they have a misunderstanding that not doing good is fine as long as it doesn't violate the law. This is the reason why self-righteousness and hypocrisy proliferate.[8]

Anybody can make a stand against great evil. But when people claim they can make a stand but in reality they do not, they compromise and end up oppressing the great good.[9]

Dickens courageously waged a battle of words against people in positions of power who should have been working in the service of common citizens and society but instead took to injustice and corruption. He declared that as long as he had the power to think and the power to speak, he would relentlessly drive out the cruelty and oppression of this world. I feel that this refusal to tolerate social iniquity finds consonance with Victor Hugo.

## Everyone's Responsibility

REES: The words of President Makiguchi carry great weight.

Harold Pinter, a leading playwright who passed away a few years ago, is also one of those citizens of great spirit and belief. When he was awarded the 2005 Nobel Prize for Literature, he was unable to attend the ceremony because he was battling against illness. Instead, a videotape that he had recorded at his home was shown. In that speech, Pinter identified the responsibilities of everyone, not just artists and poets, to "define the real truth of our lives and our societies."[10] He concluded that the obligation to do that was mandatory. His insistence that it is the responsibility of every citizen to question what the majority describes as "right," and to disobey often, is also my belief.

Of course, it takes courage to be as forthright as Harold Pinter. In this respect, I hope that our dialogue will encourage others to display their mental and physical courage in the cause of peace and justice. When political leaders behave in a cowardly fashion— as when they try to control freedom of expression and condemn the WikiLeaks activities—I hope that numerous people in many countries will question such cowardice and refuse to ally themselves with conventional, mainstream ideas and policies.

IKEDA: Without the courage to stay true to one's conviction, reforms of any kind will remain out of reach. You are a man of admirable intellect who possesses such courage and indomitable conviction.

The critical key to building peace and a society of nonviolence is for all of us, the people, to cultivate fortitude and wisdom. Furthermore, it is crucial for common citizens to strengthen bonds of solidarity while drawing forth their innate goodness to the fullest. To bring this about, I believe the time to act is now. Our actions serve as a powerful impetus for the rise of tidal forces that will usher in a new era.

# Living Up to Our Mission

IKEDA: This is a passage from *Henry VI,* the famous play by William Shakespeare:

> My crown is in my heart, not on my head;
> Not deck'd with diamonds and Indian stones,
> Nor to be seen: my crown is called content.

I was deeply moved when I first came into contact with these words many years ago. The true crown of life lies in neither power nor wealth but in the radiance within us. I have devoted myself to a peace movement based on Buddhist humanism to usher in an era enabling the crown of victory to shine in the heart of each and every unsung, uncrowned person.

In the previous conversation, we talked about Charles Dickens, who was born in Portsmouth close to where you were born. If we go back two hundred years before Dickens's time, to the end of the sixteenth century and the start of the seventeenth century, we find William Shakespeare, who left an indelible mark on the history of world literature.

The year 2011 marked the 410th anniversary of the first performance of *Hamlet*. This play, along with Shakespeare's many other works, such as *King Lear* and *Macbeth*, is still performed and loved by people around the world. Whether they are spoken by the central character or by those playing minor roles, Shakespeare's words skillfully express what lies in the heart as it moves through the gamut of emotions. Moral lessons and witty insights from life are found throughout the texts.

Shakespeare sheds a keen light on the true nature of the human being stripped of all power and vainglory. He has the magnetism to grab hold of audiences of every age and nationality. The language of truth that emanates from the soul stirs the heart to great things and summons from deep within the courage to forge on.

I have often introduced in my speeches and writings timeless insights from all ages and cultures in the hope that these precious words of wisdom will nourish the minds of young people, who shoulder responsibility for the next generation.

REES: That is reassuring. The teacher who taught me literature—great novels and plays and poetry—when I was in high school made a considerable impression because he showed the variety of insights into life that are provided by novelists and poets. Thanks to him, I began to read Shakespeare's works. That teacher showed how many of William Shakespeare's characters deplored war and instead sought love, trust, and loyalty. He also showed how they became caught up in intrigue, distrust, and betrayal.

After that, I started to seriously study poetry, including Shakespeare's plays, and I also began to write poems at that time. In my twenties and onward, I began to challenge any idea of unquestioned authority and saw poetry as a means of satirizing authoritarian characters and systems. I began to use satire to challenge bullies and to debunk those individuals who appeared to have little sense of a common humanity. In that respect, I began to develop my idea that poetry could not only be fun and humorous, it could also have a very serious side, as in challenging the use of force to solve problems. The title of my poetry anthology, *Tell Me the Truth About War*, published in 2004, represents such a challenge.

IKEDA: The copy of your anthology that you gave me has been a treasure. *Tell Me the Truth About War* has been profoundly inspiring for me, as I, too, have spoken out against the folly and cruelty of war and urged people to take action for peace. In the letter that you sent me when you presented me with your anthology, you wrote:

> The poems combine a plea for recognition of the life-enhancing attributes of humanity together with direct and indirect advocacy for an end to political leaders' fascination with militarism and other forms of violence.

This is an impassioned cry by one who knows and values the power of words.

In poetry, the power to awaken people to the truth and to sound a warning can be condensed into just a few lines. Poetry has the capacity to inspire, imbue wisdom, and elevate human beings. The wellspring of this power and capacity lies in the words *plea* and *advocacy* that you highlighted in your letter. I, too, believe that the power of words must be employed as a treasured sabre for justice, its incisive blade bared against iniquity.

The philosopher Ralph Waldo Emerson focused on these innate qualities possessed by poetry and valued the insight beating within a poem over and above meter and beauty of form. He said:

> For a verse is not a vehicle to carry a sentence as a jewel is carried in a case: the verse must be alive, and inseparable from its contents.[2]

He is the true Orpheus who writes his ode, not with syl-
lables, but men.[3]

Indeed, words resound within people's hearts only when they
are music from a brave soul.

I was intrigued by your heart-to-heart exchange with your literature teacher. Are there other episodes from your school days
that you would share?

REES: I attended an all-boys secondary school, where the teachers emphasized that each pupil should try to excel in three areas—
sports, music, and academic achievement. If you were not good at
one of those activities, you were expected to do well in the other
two.

My father's appreciation of music influenced me greatly. As I
told you before, he was lucky to be gifted with a tenor voice. He
found joy in singing, and he passed that feeling of joy to our family. My father participated many times in performances of great
choral works such as Handel's Messiah and Beethoven's Ninth
Symphony. It was a great joy for our family to go to those concerts.

I once dreamed of being able to sing like a great tenor and to do
so standing on a stage. Although it was only for a short while, I did
experience singing in a choir like my father.

Our parents often took us to concerts given by pianists and vio-
linists. Such treats began my fascination with music and theater.
We played and replayed the classics that my father enjoyed on an
old gramophone. Playing the piano at home and singing around it
were in some ways habits as well as hobbies. I also had many years
of education and training as a violinist.

I have enjoyed sports since my childhood. I used to play with
my friends in the nearby fields, organizing running races, playing
cricket and soccer; and I recall with considerable pleasure our

father taking us to Saturday afternoon soccer matches to watch our local team play.

## THE "NEVER QUIT" SPIRIT

IKEDA: It sounds as if your father played a significant role in your boyhood, opening the portals of your mind and developing your potential to take wing.

I have always urged the students of the Soka Junior and Senior High Schools in Tokyo and Kansai to recognize that, while they must of course study hard as students, it is equally vital that they extend their interests vigorously and develop their bodies and minds in a healthy, rewarding manner. Insofar as time permits, I have taken part in school events, attending concerts and chorale performances by the students and visiting exhibitions of their paintings and calligraphy. Out of my desire that the students be healthy, I used to join them in playing tennis and table tennis, doing gymnastic exercises and stretches with them.

Once, at the Festival of Health, an annual sports day at the Kansai Soka schools, one student, feeling unwell, lagged far behind everyone else in a long-distance race, the other runners reaching the finishing line one after another. He was holding his side in obvious pain but continued to soldier on with all his might. Supported by the rousing cheers of the entire school, he finally completed his run without giving up. I welcomed him at the finishing line. He was on the verge of collapsing from exhaustion, but his face glowed with the pride of not having given up. To express my utmost praise for how he had made his best effort, I took the white rosette that I was wearing and pinned it on him.

He is now working as a lawyer with strong purpose and principles. I was told that he repeatedly tried to pass the national bar examination, which ranks among the most difficult in Japan, and was on the verge of giving up at one point. But he rekindled that "never quit" spirit and passed with flying colors. Today, he is actively working for ordinary citizens and for the sake of justice.

REES: So for him, the memory of that race when he was a Soka schools student became a precious prime point for his life. Above anything else, being an educator myself, I've been impressed with the caring sentiments with which you deal with students of the Soka schools.

I remember when I visited the Soka schools in Tokyo together with the members of a delegation from the Sydney Peace Foundation in spring 2009. The performance of the *koto* orchestra at the Soka Senior High School was unforgettable. All of us were most impressed that these ancient instruments have been preserved and are still played, and with great skill and joy by those students.

Also, in our meeting with the students, lively questions were asked such as "What should we do for peace?" We felt that the students of the Soka schools were very promising with regard to their interest in social and international issues.

IKEDA: The students deepened their determination for peace through meeting with the group you led.

Along with the "never quit" spirit, the spirit of inquiry into the purpose of life and learning is central to the humanistic education adopted by the Soka schools:

> For what purpose do we cultivate wisdom?
> For what purpose do we burn with passion?
> For what purpose do we love the people?
> For what purpose do we seek a glorious future?
> For what purpose do we seek peace?[4]

Over the long course of life, people are bound to encounter various difficulties and challenges, but the Soka schools graduates are fulfilling their respective missions in life without regret, committed to developing themselves as they embrace in their hearts the question "For what purpose?" Time flies, and the students of the Soka schools' first graduating class will soon be sixty.[5]

REES: We cannot afford to lose sight of any of those questions as we strive to live as human beings. With such a spiritual foundation, the value of education shines even more brightly.

I recall that when I was in primary school, our headmistress insisted that education was the only way to make progress in life, and her views were certainly reinforced by our parents' attitudes toward life. Like my father, my mother left school early, because at that time—England during World War I—unless girls came from upper-class families, they were not expected to continue with any formal education. My mother resolved that education for her children was the way to guarantee better life chances than she had experienced.

She was a hardworking and loving individual. Although quite a petite person, she was always strong in terms of will power and values. She was determined to be even stronger when her husband was seriously injured in the war, and she courageously supported the family.

She never complained about her own lack of educational opportunity. Rather, she retained great enthusiasm for education and a burning ambition to get ahead. She gave us many examples of her enthusiasm for life: In her seventies, she enrolled in French-language classes. Then, in her eighties, she wrote and illustrated a book about the flowers, trees, and fruit bushes in her large country garden.

My mother was passionately involved in the care of the elderly. As a shrewd organizer and an imaginative leader, she enjoyed respect from people around her. Both she and my father were convinced that it was selfish to be concerned only with family interests, hence their community work. Their example certainly influenced my commitment to the principle that "the personal is the political": The conduct of personal relationships is not separate from political values and commitments.

## GIFT RELATIONSHIP

IKEDA: Many of the issues faced by society, including political issues, are caused by a pervading egotism. To remedy this prevailing problem, it is essential, as demonstrated by your parents' behavior, for each of us to illuminate the community through our example and expand the fertile ground where humanity can blossom. Yours must have been wonderful parents—a just father and a loving mother who walked the path of lifelong education, lifelong learning, and lifelong contribution.

Makiguchi, the father of Soka education, held a belief similar to your parents'. Making this belief the purpose of education, he made the following appeal:

> We should not seek the kind of egoistic happiness that is concerned only with personal happiness but is indifferent to the well-being of others. We must recognize that, while we ourselves are of course at the center of our lives, any lasting authentic security and stability will only be possible when we pursue lives of creative coexistence and mutual prosperity within society.[6]

> True happiness can only be attained when we share the joys and sorrows of others as members of society.[7]

Makiguchi considered it crucial—particularly during childhood, when the foundations for life are established—for students to learn from adults a way of life of naturally working for others and to accumulate experiences of putting this principle into action. In fact, when the Great Kanto Earthquake struck in September 1923, he called on the pupils and graduates of the elementary school where he was principal to volunteer in collecting relief supplies and delivering them to the victims. Local government officials and members of the association of headmasters looked askance as his effort, deeming it unauthorized and arbitrary. President Makiguchi was unfazed; he simply could not ignore the quake victims. That the volunteer work was meaningful could be seen in the radiant eyes of the children who participated. Essays by children at the time describe the pupils and their friends happily pulling a cart, going from door to door among the houses that had escaped harm to gather clothing and school supplies to deliver to victims.

> At first, we were rather embarrassed, but it was nothing when we realized we were doing it for people who had suffered.
>
> When we got back to school with our cart stacked with goods that we had collected in large numbers, we could not help feeling pleased even though we were children.[8]

Makiguchi advocated the ideal of *humanitarian competition* as a vision of global society to which humankind should aim. What exists at the core of this ideal is nothing but the spirit to learn and act for the happiness of both oneself and others.

REES: When a helping hand is given to others who are in difficulty or suffering, then the true value of the person as a human being appears. Social standing or position has nothing to do with that. Selfless generosity to others in difficulty displays individuals' worth and integrity.

My mother played the role of a leader serving the local community for many years, and she fulfilled her activities in the midst of looking after our family and her parents. She continued to provide unpaid service to others. In this respect, she reflected Makiguchi's ideas about humanitarian competition. I believe that these acts of selflessness are ingredients of justice. She echoed the famous line of German playwright Bertolt Brecht, "Justice is the bread of the people."[9]

For me, a sense of value built on the idea of justice preceded the ideal of peace. It's important to mention that our family conversations were often about politics, partly because our parents had strong Christian convictions about fairness and justice. The newspapers they read and the radio programs they listened to were also concerned with the politics of rebuilding a country after a world war, hence the concern with fairness to all people.

IKEDA: You have consistently engaged in service for the socially vulnerable and the tormented throughout the world. I can well understand that the point of departure for such endeavors can be found in your remarkable parents' way of life based on their convictions.

I heard that you embarked upon this worthy path of purpose and a lifetime of social contribution after graduate school. What field were you most interested in as a student? And who proved to be a significant influence at the time?

REES: I studied politics and history at university, in part because I was interested in how history influences interpretations of current events. As I pursued my studies, a historian named Charles Previté-Orton impressed me because of the depth of his scholarship and his great attention to detail, even of ancient history.

As a postgraduate student, I was inspired by Richard Titmuss, a scholar of social welfare theory. During the period of post-war reconstruction, his research and writings had considerable influence on the building of welfare state systems in European countries and also in the Soviet Union. It surprised and impressed me that a man who had no formal university education—he never obtained a degree—could be such an astute scholar and such a significant influence on his country's social policies.

One of Titmuss's influential books is *The Gift Relationship: From Human Blood to Social Policy*, a study of the international blood donor system. The "gift" refers to an act of giving without expectation of any return, let alone of a reward. Titmuss insisted that this "gift relationship"—the attitude of serving others, even those one has never met—builds the base of supportive family life, of coherent communities, and of civil societies.

IKEDA: In Buddhism, we call this kind of sincere gift *almsgiving* or *joyful giving*. Nichiren, the thirteenth-century Japanese Buddhist thinker and reformer whose teachings the Soka Gakkai members embrace, says: "If one lights a fire for others, one will brighten one's own way."[10] It holds that the more you stoke the flames of action out of your own resolve to assist others, not only will this light brighten the hearts of those around you but will reflect the dignity and illuminate the true purpose of your own life.

Given this, Toda once explained in accessible terms the way of life that Buddhist practitioners should lead:

> Becoming happy yourself is no great challenge; it's quite simple. Working for the happiness of others in addition to your own happiness, however, is the foundation of faith.[11]

REES: It is a key concept, isn't it? Professor Titmuss's conviction lies in the following point: "Social policy should always be about the triumph of altruism (unselfishness) over egoism (i.e., selfishness)."[12]

As a postgraduate student, the most significant intellectual influence on my development came from the sociologist Raymond Illsley. He gave me the opportunity to study for a doctorate and taught me methods of research. His manner of conducting his life showed that action for social justice could be combined with high standards of research and writing.

Together with these two professors, I was also influenced by the writing and activism of Saul Alinsky, who is often considered to be a founder of community organizing. He focused his organizational skills on improving the living conditions of people suffering from poverty in various parts of the United States.

IKEDA: Yes, I'm familiar with his achievements. President Obama was active as a community organizer in Chicago for some three years when he was young and has often spoken of the valuable experience he gained through working with Alinsky's successors and contributing to the local community.

Alinsky's involvement in community organizing activities was said to stem largely from seeing so many Americans living in distress in the 1930s as a result of the Great Depression, as well as his own experience of suffering from poverty. He had just graduated from university at the time, and although his academic record was excellent, he was unable to land work and barely had enough money to eat every day.

Fortunately, he was awarded a scholarship to pursue his postgraduate major in criminology. He studied the conditions of people forced into the lowest social strata. Later, while working as a criminologist at a state prison, Alinsky delved deeply into the factors driving people to commit crimes and the measures needed to prevent such situations from arising.

I understand that after you finished graduate school, you engaged in social work. You worked as a probation officer in England, and you were a supervisor of parolees serving suspended sentences in Canada. What motivated you to get involved in such work?

REES: As I continued my research at graduate school, I became interested in the ways in which people in trouble before the law could be helped instead of punished, and a social worker in my parents' hometown introduced me to a book called *Probation: the Second Chance.* As I read the book, I developed an aversion to punishment and became appalled and angry about the use of the death penalty in any country. I also realized that imprisonment had huge social and financial costs and was largely ineffective as a means of rehabilitation.

Subsequently, the British Home Office sponsored my postgraduate studies in sociology, law, social policy, psychotherapy, and social casework. My career in social work—probation, parole, and community organizing work—followed that education and training.

The comradeship, support, and humor of social worker colleagues stand out in my memory. Most of them felt that people were in trouble largely because of their lack of social skills due to a limited education, as well as difficult living conditions such as the experience of poverty.

My education and training as a social worker in London and Canada taught me that differences in social class could greatly affect people's lives; for example, determining whether individuals continued on to jail or university, where they could realize their potential. I also noticed that social systems such as law and education, which should treat all people equally, to some extent work to maintain inequality and injustice.

And I participated in the antipoverty campaign in the United States in the 1960s. I witnessed racial discrimination and the human costs of such destructiveness. I was indignant that injustices were not being challenged by mainstream politicians, but, as a relatively inexperienced frontline worker, I was not sure what strategies to use to remedy such injustices.

IKEDA: What should we do to fundamentally resolve poverty and human rights violations, which cause so many people to suffer? The only solution is that ordinary people, every one of us, must awaken to the truth and take united action. This is what Alinsky advocated, and your own endeavors are an extension of this belief.

In *Reveille for Radicals*, which summarized his activist experiences, Alinsky writes:

> The enormous power necessary for the development of democracy and the resolving of those issues which make life unhappy and insecure can come only from an organization of all of the People's Organizations, institutions, and the people themselves.[13]

> It is impossible to overemphasize the enormous importance of people's doing things themselves.[14]

> It is living in dignity to achieve things through your own intelligence and efforts. It is living as a human being.[15]

I feel a profound resonance with these insights.

REES: All of these words symbolize the core of Alinsky's philosophy. He considered it essential for people to be proactive in applying their capabilities to create a society in which the dignity of a human being is fulfilled, where equality, justice, and freedom are promoted. He also urged people to win one step at a time for a better future through their own power.

IKEDA: Which is why Alinsky found fascism, which rides roughshod over the people, utterly intolerable. As the ultimate bulwark against its resurgence, he strove to forge bonds of solidarity and trust among awakened citizens.

In Japan some eighty years ago (in 1930), when militarism began to rear its ugly head, Makiguchi, by publishing *The System of Value-Creating Pedagogy*,[16] sounded a warning to a society plunging into turmoil and instability:

> The more powerful the corrupt grow, the more they persecute the good—who, in contrast, remain forever isolated and vulnerable. As the former expands in power and influence, the latter contracts. Under such conditions, society cannot but become an increasingly threatening and dangerous place.[17]

With this warning, he, along with his disciple, Toda, founded the Soka Kyoiku Gakkai (Value-Creating Education Society), later to become the Soka Gakkai.

Social evils such as war cannot be deterred by theory and logic alone. My two mentors thus sought to establish solidarity among people who strive for the kind of peace and justice that cannot be undermined. This was the spirit with which they founded the Soka Gakkai.

Makiguchi once counseled an aspiring young actor by asking, "What do you think of the great drama of life, which eclipses any work of fiction?" He hoped to encourage the actor to see that the highest purpose in life was to guide suffering people on the stage of life—the real world filled with distress and difficulty—to a life of peace and happiness.

We, the SGI members, have inherited the spirit of Makiguchi and Toda, and expanded the solidarity of awakened people to 192 countries and territories throughout the world. As good citizens, we are striving to broaden the circle of hope and encouragement in our respective communities while promoting peace, culture, and education, working with like-minded organizations worldwide. Our goal is to continue collaborating with you and people of insight around the world who are also striving to advance happiness for both oneself and others. We will engage with all our might in a empowerment movement of the people, by the people, for the people.

# Spiritual Struggle

IKEDA: Diversity is a source of abundant energy. The dynamism and manifold wonders of Australia, the "land of diversity," emerge from its various cultures as they draw inspiration from one another, sometimes even melding with one another.

In January 2000, the same year that Sydney, Australia, hosted the Summer Olympic Games and Paralympic Games, I met Ms. Le Hoa Lam, then the mayor of Auburn City in the Sydney Metropolitan Area, at Soka University of Japan. Auburn City is the site of the Sydney Olympic Park. Ms. Lam hails from Vietnam and, in her childhood, fled the war in her country. After undergoing great adversity, she immigrated first to Malaysia, then to Canada, and finally to Australia.

I understand that more than half the population of Auburn City were born overseas like Ms. Lam, who is imbued with the unfettered spirit of global citizenship and thus symbolizes her city, which strives to be a community of creative coexistence and harmony. We have our SGI-Australia Culture Centre in the Sydney Olympic Park in Auburn City. Our members come from a wide variety of cultural backgrounds and work to better their communities and society in general as exemplary citizens. Australia, with its broad cultural diversity, is a great country of hope brimming with infinite potential.

When did you leave the United Kingdom, where you were born, to reside in Australia, the land of hope?

REES: It was 1978, just before the election of UK Prime Minister Margaret Thatcher's first government. I was working at the University of Aberdeen in Scotland at the time.

At that university, Professor Raymond Illsley, who was my academic mentor (see Conversation Two), created one of the largest social science research units in Europe. I stayed on at Aberdeen for a while after obtaining my doctorate there, and during that time, I came to hear that a professor was being sought by the Faculty of Arts and Social Sciences at the University of Sydney to fill the Chair of Social Work.

In those days, the position of professor in major United Kingdom and Australian universities could only be by appointment following widespread advertising and subsequent international competition, hence the challenge from my colleagues to apply for such a position. I did so and was appointed. Coming to Australia and to the country's oldest university seemed like a new adventure. In some ways, it still is.

In fact, my brother's migration to Australia many years earlier had some influence on my migration to this country about ten years later.

IKEDA: There was a deep connection from the start.

Nearly half a century has passed since I visited the enchanting land of Australia, in May 1964, which was somewhat earlier than when your brother moved there. The first place I visited was Sydney. During my six-day stay, I also visited Melbourne, Brisbane, and the renowned Gold Coast to encourage the pioneering SGI members outside Sydney.

The coastline that seemed to stretch on forever with its beautiful sandy beaches was spectacular, and the sparkling waves that lapped the shore remain in my mind's eye. It is a superb place, and I fondly recall feeling that I wanted to go back there one day, thinking how much our Soka Gakkai youth would love this place.

During my stay, I was interviewed by the Australian Broadcasting Corporation. I understand you worked for ABC as a radio broadcaster for several years.

REES: My radio interviews addressed the means and meaning of peace with justice. Alongside my peace research work, I have kept up my efforts to raise public awareness of peace through those radio programs.

Needless to say, the mass media as represented by television, radio, and the newspapers have a strong influence on people. However, much of the material contained in the media is truculent, somewhat preoccupied with violent events.

Violence in the media is partly inherited from the Hollywood tradition, which assumes that violence attracts an audience. The brutality of the American gun culture somehow spills over into the practice of aggressive interviewing and the encouragement of racist and fundamentalist points of view, often in complete contravention of the principles of human rights. Of course, there are Australian and Japanese imitations of such US media culture.

To challenge this culture, leaders in education, in politics, religion, journalism, and the arts need to emphasize that quality of life comes almost entirely from the language and practice of nonviolence. Stories of nonviolence and of social justice are waiting to be told. Such stories, and the humanity that they express, can replace the accounts of violence that appear to be the mainstay of so many media outlets. Radio and television programs about the history of peace and nonviolence can replace the fascination with films that glorify war.

A history of the cultural and educational achievements of the SGI—in particular, the spiritual struggles carried out based on nonviolence by the Soka Gakkai leaders Tsunesaburo Makiguchi, Josei Toda, and you, President Ikeda, as well as the examples of Mahatma Gandhi and Dr. Martin Luther King Jr.—needs to be told.

IKEDA: I appreciate your understanding of our movement and its ideals. Transforming public attitudes about violence, as you have identified, is an urgent issue. I hold in the highest esteem your work to elevate awareness of peace by promoting the ideals of nonviolence. The SGI is, likewise, a movement that seeks to bring hearts together by offering encouragement to countless people with words of hope and words of courage.

It was while visiting your country in 1964 that I first proposed an English-language newspaper in the United States, the first Soka Gakkai publication overseas, following our daily paper in Japan, the *Seikyo Shimbun,* which launched in 1951. The English organ was named the *World Tribune* with the aim of protecting the people with words of justice and a vow to create world peace. The name was derived from tribunes, individuals who defended the common people from the tyrannical aristocracy of ancient Rome. Members in the United States led the preparations and, three months later, in August 1964, the first issue was published. Since then, we have published periodicals on all continents—Asia, Oceania, Europe, Africa, North America, and South America. They now exceed fifty.

From country to country, there is a wide array of titles: In Canada, the organ is called *New Century*; in the Philippines, *Pagasa* (Hope); and in Italy, *Il Nuovo Rinascimento* (the New Renaissance). The magazine published by SGI-Australia is called *Indigo*.

We are grateful for the instructive essays and other writings you have contributed to the magazine.

REES: That magazine and your other publications must now discuss the consequences of the catastrophes that hit Japan in March 2011: the earthquake, the tsunami, and the dangers of radiation from the destruction at the Fukushima Nuclear Power Plant. Those catastrophes have resulted in a humanitarian crisis and challenge for the people of Japan. In that respect, your magazines and newspapers will have a crucial responsibility to keep the public well informed and give them hope. But I understand that it's never easy to keep magazines and newspapers alive in the digital age, even when those publications are faced with huge responsibilities in a time of national crisis.

IKEDA: Publishing a newspaper is indeed a grueling enterprise. I remember the numerous challenges that Toda and I had to grapple with in launching the *Seikyo Shimbun* more than sixty years ago. Initially, there was only a small staff; I was then in my twenties and engaged in editorial work under Toda's direction. Among my fond memories from that time are introducing the paper to people in our neighborhood and delivering it on foot.

Ceaseless effort and creative thinking are essential to infuse a newspaper with dynamic energy. Since its launch, *Seikyo Shimbun* articles have been edited with the belief that the paper, by providing a discourse on humanistic principles, would be fulfilling its social purpose.

In general, newspapers have a crucial role to provide extensive coverage of events and situations, identifying issues and sounding alarms to rectify them. On the other hand, one cannot deny that they can have the tendency to focus excessively on the dark, negative aspects of human society.

The *Seikyo Shimbun* has continued to send out messages of hope and courage by shining a light on the goodness of individuals who work for the sake of society. All human beings are endowed with boundless potential and intrinsically possess the expansive capacity to prevail over every ordeal and challenge. Only the nameless multitudes can bring about the transformation of an era, creating a better society.

Following the Great East Japan Earthquake (in March 2011), the *Seikyo Shimbun* devoted every effort and resource to voicing solidarity with the survivors who are rising to confront this unprecedented tragedy. Many people who read the *Seikyo Shimbun* in stricken communities have voiced their gratitude, saying it provided them with strength and sustained their will to carry on in the days after the calamity.

The mission statement of the *Seikyo Shimbun* is to contribute to the happiness of people and the development of society, and to advance peace in the world. The paper will continue to return to this point of departure as it strives to enhance and improve the quality of its articles.

Toda's words still ring in my ears. Speaking about the newspaper industry, he said: "I am well aware that the world is an unhappy place, but these papers do not suggest at all how to make it any happier. The *Seikyo Shimbun*, however, does write about how one can become happy. There is no other newspaper like it."[1] Taking his words to heart, I have continued contributing pieces like the serialized novel *The New Human Revolution* and various essays to the *Seikyo Shimbun*.

REES: That is truly wonderful. It is also what I feel when I read your annual peace proposals. You write as though you are a young man: energetic, optimistic, almost always poetic. You hope for and write about the best of all possible worlds. That's inspiring.

The *Seikyo Shimbun* and other SGI publications are supported by the spirit to strive for a more peaceful, happier, and more humanistic society from among many possibilities in the world, and your own actions are based on the same spirit.

## INDIGENOUS PEOPLE

IKEDA: January 26, Australia Day (commemorating the founding of the nation) also happens to be the day we commemorate the founding of the SGI. I feel this is a wondrous coincidence and demonstrates a special affinity with your country.

Australia is one of the most popular destinations for Japanese people. In recent years, some 400,000 Japanese have been visiting your country annually for sightseeing, business, study abroad, training programs, and so forth. When I visited, there was not even a direct flight to connect the two countries, and the era of bilateral exchanges had not yet come into being, so it feels like a different world today.

Among all the sister-city arrangements that local governments in Japan have entered into around the world, Australia accounts for one of the largest numbers—exceeded only by the United States, China, and South Korea—with more than 100 Australian partners to date.

I heard that "Australia" comes from *Terra Australis Incognita*, Latin for the *Unknown Land of the South*. Since the time of the ancient Greeks, it was believed that a vast undiscovered continent existed somewhere in the Southern Hemisphere like the Northern Hemisphere. When Europeans began to arrive in the seventeenth century, they named Australia after this legendary continent.

What was the biggest difference in the natural environment and climate that you discovered when you moved from the United Kingdom, an island nation in the Northern Hemisphere, to the vast continental country of Australia?

Rees: The first thing I felt about living in Sydney was that it is indeed a place blessed with bright sunshine—a complete contrast to the grey skies of London. The weather is warm throughout most of the year, but there is usually significant rainfall.

Above all, the greatest difference is that the seasons are inverted from what they are in the Northern Hemisphere. December, when Christmas is celebrated, is in the cold winter season in the case of the United Kingdom and Japan. But it is midsummer in Australia. So, we can see Santa Claus in town wearing shorts and a short-sleeved shirt! Also, in Australia, the sunny part of the room faces north, and the north wind is warmer.

Ikeda: In that case, the storyline in Aesop's fable *The North Wind and the Sun* changes, does it not?[2] The traveler would be too warm and would take off his cloak when the North Wind blows!

In recent years, Australians have been taking advantage of this difference by visiting Japan in increasing numbers for summer skiing holidays in places like Hokkaido (when it is winter there). My Hokkaido friends have a deep fondness for Australians. Bilateral friendship and mutual understanding will deepen as exchanges progress in these ways.

A great scenic area in Australia, famous and popular among the Japanese, is the Great Barrier Reef, the world's largest coral reef, located on the coastline of the State of Queensland. Your country is also known for its many UNESCO (United Nations Educational, Scientific and Cultural Organization) World Heritage natural sites (see Conversation Eight), such as the Lord Howe Island Group and Fraser Island.

Rees: Australia is full of breathtakingly beautiful places like Fraser Island. In particular, I never cease to be amazed by the natural beauty of the Great Barrier Reef. Having seen other great natural wonders of the world—such as the Grand Canyon—I thought that the Barrier Reef might not live up to my expectations. It exceeded them. Turquoise waters, fish species in all the colors of the rainbow, and numerous varieties of coral provide a fantastic undersea home, an underworld that is more amazing than might be imagined in one's wildest dreams.

However, my greatest sense of wonder is for the country's red center—Uluru. Although Uluru measures approximately six miles in circumference, it was formed as one single rock 600 million years ago by sedimentation on the ocean bed. Its present formation is said to have been sculpted by erosion and weathering over more than 400 million years. It contains a large amount of iron, and its surface is oxidized, thereby bringing about its reddish-brown color. Its color changes from hour to hour between brown, red, and black according to the sun's rays.

Any reflective human being standing in that vast desert area is bound to feel both respectful and grateful for the momentum of the past and the legacy of the Alcheringa, the Dreamtime of Indigenous Australians: respectful of their stewardship of the ancient lands, grateful to be seeing and breathing this hub of Australian existence. I make the latter point despite the original and false European account of Australia's origins—that the land was discovered by Captain Cook! That is to say, the landing and exploration by the British naval captain James Cook in 1770 was never the beginning of Australia. Ancestors of the Aboriginal people were living there far back in the distant past—it is said from at least 50,000 years ago.

IKEDA: Unfortunately, I have never visited either the Great Barrier Reef or Uluru, but I can almost visualize their stunning appearance just from your descriptions. Uluru, of course, used to be known as Ayers Rock, but I've heard that the ancient name has become widely accepted since ownership of the land was returned to the Aboriginal peoples in 1985.

Aboriginal peoples have visited this sacred site since ancient times. They consider it to be the source of life—here, they draw energy from nature and feel their ancestors' breath mix with their own in the space between heaven and earth.

Indigenous Australian culture is said to be among the oldest continuous cultures in the world. By coexisting in harmony with nature, the Aboriginal people have developed a worldview in which human beings, animals, and plants are all connected by strong bonds of life. They offer a vital perspective in the modern age, where the destruction of our natural environment continues.

In May 2005, we welcomed to Soka University and the Soka Junior and Senior High Schools a party led by Dr. Joan Winch, founder of the Perth Aboriginal Medical Service at the Marr Mooditj college, who has dedicated herself to safeguarding and preserving the indigenous culture of the Nyungar community in Western Australia. Students, including the members of the South Pacific Research Group, had the chance to meet with Dr. Winch's delegation. My hope is that the occasion served as an important pillar of bilateral goodwill and will lead to further exchanges, especially youth exchanges, in the future.

REES: I feel exactly the same. I was once engaged for about six years in activities in the State Council for Reconciliation in New South Wales and used to travel from Sydney to various places initiating and participating in dialogue about community issues that caused controversy between Aboriginal and non-Aboriginal citizens. Through that experience, I discovered that dialogue went smoothly over matters of common threat to their livelihood, such as environmental destruction. Initially, I would identify the differences between Aboriginal and non-Aboriginal culture, so I felt above all the need to discuss people's understanding of the respective cultures and traditions.

In that sense, I have always considered that the life and work of the Australian poet Judith Wright is distinguished by her commitment to the welfare of indigenous people and to the protection of the environment. Her close relationship with the Aboriginal poet Oodgeroo Noonuccal characterizes her love of the values and traditions of the Aboriginal peoples. Simultaneously, she also wrote of the inspiration derived from observing the natural environment.

For example, the poem *Flame Tree* puts across how Wright was struck by the energy and colors of the bright red flame tree:

How to live, I said, as the flame-tree lives?
—to know what the flame-tree knows; to be
prodigal of my life as that wild tree
and wear my passion so?

What the earth takes of her it will restore.
These are the thanks of lovers who share one mind.[3]

Through the energy of life that lives in the flame tree, Wright sends a message to readers of her passion for life and requests they not hesitate to express such passion, conveying the message to be passionate about humanity and the vast universe.

IKEDA: The poetic mind to appreciate the wonderment and vibrancy of life in nature on such a profound level is precisely what people need in this modern age. Judith Wright is read widely, and not just in the English-speaking world, as she had been translated into various languages. A collection of her poems has also been published in Japan. Born on a ranch in the northeast corner of New South Wales, Wright grew up in the remote countryside, where it took several hours to travel from her house to her nearest neighbor.

Her poetry reveals a deep sense of empathy with and appreciation for nature:

> Lock your branches around me, tree;
> let the harsh, wooden scales of bark enclose me.
> Take me into your life and smother me with bloom. . . .[4]

> I wait for the rising of a star
> whose spear of light shall transfix me—
> of a far-off world whose silence
> my very truth must answer.[5]

A firm advocate of the need to protect the environment and a dedicated activist toward this end, Wright established the Wildlife Preservation Society of Queensland and was a member of the Australian Conservation Committee. At present, there are more than 550 national parks and some 6,000 wildlife sanctuaries in your country, in addition to the UNESCO World Heritage sites. I also understand that initiatives to protect endangered species and ecosystems are being implemented under the National Reserve System.

Australians are very much aware of nature and the need for environmental protection, with some 800,000 people participating as members of more than a thousand conservation groups. Natural conservation is an important issue in Japan, too, and I feel that there is much to learn from Australia's far-reaching undertaking.

CONVERSATION FOUR

# Identity and Globalization

IKEDA: Australian Prime Minister Julia Gillard visited Japan in April 2011. She was the first foreign head of government to visit the area struck by the earthquake and subsequent tsunami. In Minamisanriku, Miyagi Prefecture, Prime Minister Gillard gave toy koalas to children as she encouraged disaster victims. The newspapers and television news covered this extensively, moving the hearts of many Japanese.

Australia has been generous with its support, from the dispatch of a large search-and-rescue team immediately after the earthquake to setting up a new program to welcome students and educators to Australia from the disaster areas. People throughout Japan are grateful for the profound friendship and goodwill of the Australian government and citizenry. We will never forget this kindness. I am convinced that, in the future, a succession of young people from the stricken areas will come of age and reach out in friendship to Australia, serving as bridges to further goodwill.

REES: This visit to Japan by the Australian prime minister reminds us, once again, about the interdependence of all people, in particular in times of tragedy, such as the devastation and human loss in your country. Acts of generosity in service to others are crucial parts of the bridge building that you and I have been discussing in this dialogue about peace and justice. I'm glad that Prime Minister Gillard showed courage and friendship by visiting Japan at a time when it would perhaps have been easier to stay away. Thanks for your observations about the significance of her visit.

IKEDA: We are the ones to thank you. Australia has been building a new model of coexistence and harmony as a multicultural nation that prizes diversity. As one effort toward that end, I know that national policy encourages pupils to learn a language in addition to English, the official language, starting from the elementary-school level. A wide range of languages, including Japanese, French, German, Italian, Greek, Spanish, Arabic, Chinese, Indonesian, and Malay, are all taught in the classroom. This is truly international.

It is also gratifying to hear that the number of people learning Japanese in Australia is one of the largest in the world. Timboon P-12, a unified school program in the State of Victoria that includes primary and secondary school education, has conducted exchanges with our Kansai Soka Junior and Senior High Schools for many years. Many students at Timboon have opted to study Japanese and visit Japan as part of the curriculum. Learning a foreign language is an important first step in understanding a different culture, a profoundly meaningful challenge.

Australia adopted its policy of multiculturalism in 1973, and various reforms have been implemented in subsequent years. Can you explain some of the historical context behind these endeavors?

REES: Although Australia is a migrant country, and although we continue to admit our quota of new migrants and a small number of refugees, Australia's past policies were neither generous nor welcoming. In the first half of the twentieth century, the

White Australia Policy¹—premised on the notion that the country should be populated only by people from Britain and other Anglo Saxon parts of Europe—encouraged a suspicion of "the other," of people who were neither white nor Christian, who appeared to have strange food, clothes, religions, and customs. This suspicion of "the other" continues as a current in Australian society, even though the numerous people who support asylum seekers and refugees are always challenging conservative and prejudiced attitudes.

Our diversity of people, customs, and cultures has made Australia a far more dynamic, far more interesting country than during the period when politicians wanted a homogeneous population—white Anglo Saxons only. Tolerance for multicultural diversity can produce understanding and a respect for the interdependence of all peoples. Australia has become far more interesting on account of new citizens' foods, music, dress, religions, films, architecture, and respect for hard work.

A large part of Australia's economy depends on the industry and imagination of new migrants. Australia's multicultural, multiethnic society has been built on an ability to integrate new customs and on acquiring a tolerance for difference. When this tolerance is converted into an appreciation of different people and customs, a new dynamic appears.

IKEDA: Australia's youthful energy toward the future is vibrant.

The University of Sydney, where you have taught many students, has been a venue for exchanges with different cultures and philosophies since its early days. A great deal is owed to James Murdoch for forming close ties between Australia and Japan, as he was instrumental as the professor in charge of establishing the Department of Oriental Studies. He was born in Scotland and studied at your alma mater, the University of Aberdeen, before immigrating to Australia. After that, he taught English and history at schools in Japan for more than twenty years, starting in 1889. The students he taught include the great novelist Soseki Natsume and Kijuro Shidehara, a prime minister of Japan.

After Murdoch moved to Australia (at the request of the Australian government), two Japanese he selected became engaged in Japanese language education at the University of Sydney and other establishments. One of them, Mitsuji Koide, studied under Inazo Nitobe, who served as under-secretary-general of the League of Nations. Nitobe came from Iwate Prefecture, which was among the areas stricken by the recent calamity. In his youth, Nitobe, aspiring to himself be a bridge across the Pacific Ocean, studied in the United States. He had close ties with Makiguchi as well.

Nitobe encouraged young people following in his footsteps to venture abroad. However, his exhortations in no way constituted an endorsement of the kind of colonial policies being promoted at the time; he urged his protégés to emigrate out of purely peaceful reasons. Koide's move to Australia to promote Japanese language education is said to have been largely due to Nitobe's influence.

Nitobe recorded his belief as follows:

> At a time when there are increasing opportunities for East and West to meet, if they confront one another with hostility or a suspicious mind they will be unable to grasp the truth of each other and their misunderstanding will deepen, and there is a danger that wretchedness will arise in their diplomatic relations.

> We should stand on common ground as human beings with no preconceived notions, discarding superficial circumstances and formalities. We should strive for international understanding, and advancing such understanding is the task facing the people of our country now and in the

future. Surely it is the duty of Japanese people to build a bridge between East and West.[2]

Nitobe's call for an open mentality assumes increasing importance in the age of globalization, which requires improved dialogue to promote mutual understanding.

REES: My years as a social worker in different countries and my work in social justice taught me that conflicts are usually about people's sense of identity. Their search for identity always raises questions that can be answered through dialogue. Such questions include, "Will you take me seriously?" "Will you respect my views even if you disagree with them?" and "Will you find the space and time to listen to my needs?" Long before I participated in peace negotiations, these everyday experiences polished my skills in dialogue and my appreciation of its importance.

Whenever I think about this, the behavior of the former president of South Africa, Nelson Mandela, comes to mind. Meeting him face to face, he conveys humor, a genuine interest in others' welfare, a disregard for his own interests, and a certain incredulity that human beings can be cruel to one another. Therefore, his gentle disbelief about human rights abuses and about resorting to violence is expressed without any obvious antagonism toward those with whom he disagrees. He conveys a certain majesty and dignity. In addition, he has always asked "Why?"—a question aimed at unmasking reasons for violence, at identifying the causes of injustice.

IKEDA: I, too, respect and deeply admire him. I will always remember how his face was etched with compassion and that he never failed to warmly embrace those around him like a spring breeze. I first met Mr. Mandela in Tokyo in October 1990. It was soon after his release from prison, where he spent some 10,000 days in indescribable struggle and hardship. Yet he overcame his ordeal in triumph.

Our discussion turned to promoting exchanges between South Africa and Japan, and he was delighted when I told him I would welcome students from South Africa to Soka University of Japan. I recall his secretary, Ismail Meer, who was also present, said that they were grateful for how the invitation recognized African students as human beings, the same recognition that was denied them during the years they suffered under apartheid. Meer's candor struck me deeply.

Soka University of Japan has exchange agreements with numerous universities in Africa, including in Egypt, Ghana, Kenya, Senegal, and South Africa. In addition, Soka University offers instruction in Swahili, and more than 1,000 students take African studies courses every year.

I am pleased that the promises we made to Mr. Mandela have been bearing fruit year by year. Exchanges among young people open new paths of friendship. As you point out, the key lies in action based on profound insight into the nature of human beings and on a firm philosophical basis, such as that held by Mr. Mandela.

Among President Mandela's words that I have taken to heart are these: "Education is the most powerful weapon we can use to change the world."[3] The key importance of education was also among the topics we discussed when I met you and Dame Leonie Kramer, then the chancellor of the University of Sydney, in November 2000. I remember clearly her concern that, while it conveys a great deal of knowledge, modern education may be falling short in terms of teaching students to be better human beings.

REES: I cannot help but feel that there are two big dangers affecting universities around the globe. The first concerns the trend to think that universities are really businesses first, and that their role as educational institutions is secondary. This assumption leads to a preoccupation with fundraising, charging students more for less, and expecting staff to teach in larger classes and to justify their existence by competing for scarce research funds. This is a toxic trend that I strongly oppose.

The second danger derives from the trend I have mentioned: It concerns the notion that efficient management is a key to a university's success and to the conduct of students' subsequent careers. In this way, imagination, creativity, and the ability to break down conventional limitations are discouraged. Managerialism that values obedience and efficiency—how to cut costs and produce more—takes over. I strongly oppose such managerialism. Unless this malady is beaten down, universities cannot pursue their fundamental mission to nurture humanity.

IKEDA: Currently, with the birth rate and the number of children declining in Japan, the operating environment for university administrations is becoming increasingly adverse. It is imperative that careful attention be paid to the points about which you express concern.

For whom do universities exist in the first place? I have repeatedly stated that they exist for those people who could not themselves go to university. To be granted the opportunity to receive a higher education is itself an extraordinary social privilege. An untold number of people want to attend university but are denied that choice. I believe that people who have been fortunate to receive such an education have an obligation to repay that privilege by working on behalf of those less fortunate.

This was also the belief of my mentors, Makiguchi and Toda, for Soka pedagogy is an educational model for the development of well-rounded human beings. During his time as a primary school principal, Makiguchi pioneered a broad range of educational reforms, including an effort to encourage children from poor areas to attend school by providing them free lunches.

While studying abroad, Nitobe was also pained by the plight of the large numbers of children who could not attend school due to poverty and family circumstances. After returning to Japan, he established a night school in Sapporo, Hokkaido. He advocated the establishment of a "university for the people" that would be open to those who could not attend university for financial and other reasons. This commitment to humanistic education was something he and Makiguchi shared.

REES: In Australia, there are many people who enter university after having had experience in society. Nearly 40 percent of students throughout the whole country are twenty-five years old or older. Many universities are positive about accepting mature students and provide a range of support, such as setting up systems to prepare them for university entrance, which are called bridging programs. Soka University, founded by you, has since its early days been widening the path of education for people of all ages through distance learning.

IKEDA: The launch of a correspondence education division was one of the major goals from the time I pledged to establish Soka University. The source of this determination dates back to the correspondence courses for young women that Makiguchi developed at the beginning of the twentieth century. Also, the first thing that Toda embarked upon after World War II was to provide a correspondence program for young people who, because of the war, were unable to study even if they wanted to. Having inherited this spirit, we set our sights on launching a correspondence education division at the same time as the start of Soka University, aiming to create a university that was open to the people, to everyone. At first, we were unable to obtain accreditation because our request was unprecedented. But in 1976, the year after the first students graduated from Soka University, we were able to launch our long-awaited Division of Correspondence Education.

More than thirty-five years have passed since then, and now the community of Soka University correspondence education alumni has spread not only throughout Japan but throughout the world. The annual summer session is attended by students of all ages, from the young to the elderly, who travel from the United States, Canada, the United Kingdom, France, Germany, China, South Korea, Thailand, Singapore, and Australia. It has become a program for citizens of all walks of life to come together as schoolmates.

Enrollment in the correspondence division is currently the largest in Japan, and the division is continuing to develop steadily. Many graduates are now successful professionals contributing in their chosen fields, having obtained doctorates or become attorneys, certified public accountants, or certified tax accountants. By serving in their respective posts, these alumni represent bright beacons of hope for society.

To honor their great journey in life, I composed for them a poem, *Glorious Philosophers of Life! Light of Learning for the New Century!* Allow me to quote a few lines:

> With eyes searching for the truth,
> blazing fervently,
> we gaze upon that infinitude of learning.

> The flower of our life
> is to live out a meaningful existence
> without cease or let up.
> For us there is no need
> for words of formality.

So, we shall study with pride
even when we are a hundred.
Victory, glory and honor
are not determined by age.
The spirit to master knowledge
is itself Victory.[4]

REES: It is interesting that you should quote from a poem to express the value of education as the surest means of building a more just, more life-enhancing, and visionary world. To be a poet and to craft poetry, you need that extra perspective that encourages people's imagination and hopes. A passion for education is, in a way, a commitment to a poetry of existence that opens all sorts of possibilities for freedom of expression, for spiritual, political, and cultural understanding. In that respect, perhaps our dialogue should concentrate on the contents of inspiring poets and poems? Such a fascination with the poetry of existence would contribute to lifelong learning.

IKEDA: I agree wholeheartedly. Let's discuss this subject in greater depth as our dialogue proceeds.

Speaking of lifelong learning, Murdoch, whom we mentioned above, was more than fifty when he started to learn Japanese. Living in Japan for many years, he grew interested in how Japan had managed to reach parity with Western countries in just a few decades following the Meiji Restoration, which led him to study Japanese history in earnest. However, the only writings on the history of Japan prior to the arrival of the Portuguese in the sixteenth century were in Japanese. So, he made up his mind to learn the language, starting with the *Iroha* Syllabary, an old Japanese alphabet. He then read through such Japanese classics as the *Kojiki* (Record of Ancient Matters) and *Man'yoshu* (Collection of Ten Thousand Leaves), and studied as many historical documents as he could. The result was the publication of volume one of his masterpiece, *A History of Japan*, the first volume reaching more than 700 pages.

Natsume, Murdoch's student, described the significance of this work in a newspaper review:

> Magazines in the West usually include advertisements for one or two written works about Japan a week. In recent times, collecting all these books would easily enable one to fill a significant library. However, it is not too much to say that it is extremely rare to come across a tome that is compiled from genuine observation, genuine effort, genuine sympathy and genuine research. I am pleased to have the opportunity to introduce to the Japanese people this rare work of history that has been written by my teacher.[5]

The review was published in 1910, a century ago. Nowadays, our means of learning about other countries have increased dramatically. Unfortunately, efforts to understand different cultures and histories on a mutual basis remain far from adequate. It is vital that we expand the opportunities for people to communicate face to face and engage in heart-to-heart exchanges.

## Building Trust Isn't Easy

REES: There are things that I have felt strongly when carrying out research, travelling to places for conflict resolution around the world. The first point is the importance of learning about a country's history and something about the biography of the persons with whom one engages in dialogue. This concern with history and biography usually displays a certain respect that is appreciated by the other country, by the other participants in dialogue.

The second point is that, following such concern with history and biography, it is important to develop personal understanding and subsequent trust. But trust does not come easily. It requires several steps and the realization that even when trust is achieved, it may be lost very quickly and will have to be regained. Because of that, it is difficult to build trust. Our absolute resolve to build trust is required, whatever difficulties we may face, whatever temporary deterioration there may be in relationships, and even though there will be setbacks.

IKEDA: These are both important points. I readily agree with you in light of my own experiences. I'd add that artistic and cultural exchanges are indispensable in establishing heartfelt rapport.

In February 1993, while I was visiting the United States, I received an inquiry from the office of the president of Colombia asking whether I was willing to go through with a planned visit to Colombia. Tensions in that country were running high after a series of terrorist bombings. My intentions remained unchanged; I replied that I would visit Colombia with the same spirit of courage displayed by the Colombian people.

I was to arrive at the Colombian capital of Bogotá to participate in the opening of "Eternal Treasures of Japan," an exhibition cosponsored by the Tokyo Fuji Art Museum, which I founded. Three years earlier, the "Great Cultural Exhibition of Colombia," featuring works of art and artifacts of Colombia, had been held at the Tokyo Fuji Art Museum with wholehearted cooperation from many people, particularly the Colombian ambassador to Japan at the time. First Lady Carolina Isakson de Barco flew all the way from Colombia to Japan to attend the opening ceremony. The exhibition was a great success, attracting widespread interest.

The "Eternal Treasures of Japan" exhibition in Colombia was in part our way of replying to such goodwill. Responding to sincerity with sincerity is the spirit I inherited from my mentor. And it assumes an even greater importance if the act of sincerity is extended at a time when people are facing one of the most difficult times in their life. This is the true way people should live.

At the opening ceremony in Bogotá, I promised to further expand friendship between the two countries, expressing my belief that the solidarity of people through cultural exchange was the path that humanity must follow in order to prevail over barbarism. Although such exchanges have been humble and largely overlooked, we of the SGI have managed to compile a meaningful record of exchange with many countries.

REES: I understood that your establishment of the Tokyo Fuji Art Museum was nothing short of action based on poetic inspiration. That great achievement clarifies the appeal of the true nature inherent in great art to enrich our lives, and it tells the story of the dignity of the artist's spirituality and creativity.

Artists break down the walls of habitual practice and promote visions of world citizenship. In this way, they touch the hearts and minds of so many people. They also show the courage of their convictions. By their art, they make public their views.

Through works of art that are a sublimation of the spirit, artists contribute to a dialogue that transcends countries and cultures. When my students from all over the world study the poets who strive for peace and social justice, the students discover that in all their countries, powerful protests against injustice, against authoritarian rule, against human rights abuses, have been made by artists, composers, musicians, and poets. For those reasons, I was enthusiastic about the works displayed in the Tokyo Fuji Art Museum.

IKEDA: As museum founder, let me express my deep gratitude for your warm understanding of its activities.

As you said, art elevates the human spirit and possesses great potential to unite people's hearts. I am convinced that the more we respect the arts and other facets of the world's diverse cultures, and the more we pursue exchange, the more progress we will achieve toward what could be called "globalization of the human heart."

During my Colombia visit, I had a friendly discussion with César Gaviria Trujillo, who in 1990 had succeeded President Virgilio Barco Vargas as president. President Gaviria stressed that he would like the leaders, people, and intellectuals of Japan to understand that Colombia is a land of great variety and diversity. In other words, although his country faced serious challenges such as terrorist attacks, those challenges did not represent the real Colombia. Rather than being distracted by such issues, he wanted us to see Colombia as it truly is, a country blessed with great natural splendor and rich in resources. He was still in his forties and was soon to bear the weight of an entire country on his shoulders, his strong sense of responsibility evident.

I spoke with equal candor:

> One cannot discern the truth merely by observing surface appearances. We need to ascertain matters from the standpoint of the other person, seeing things with our own eyes. Firmly grounded efforts to improve mutual understanding are especially crucial in an age of increasing globalization.

President Gaviria nodded in agreement.

The march of time is inexorable, with the second decade of the twenty-first century already upon us, and I have grown to feel even more strongly about the point I made.

CONVERSATION FIVE

# A Law for Life

REES: My dialogue with you so far has been characterized by our commitment to the philosophy, language, and practice of nonviolence. Mahatma Gandhi called such a philosophy a law for life.

Sadly, the man who murdered almost eighty people in Norway (on July 22, 2011)[1] was completely unfamiliar with such a vision, such a way of life. In consequence, a whole nation grieves, and numerous families must adjust to the awful loss of someone they loved dearly.

This catastrophe in Norway is personal to me, as my wife, Ragnhild, is Norwegian. By natural temperament and as a result of the peace-loving culture from which she comes, she has always been committed to peace with justice, to universal human rights, and to nonviolence in all its forms. There is such a contrast between those beliefs and what has recently happened.

IKEDA: The car bombing and indiscriminate shooting constituted a savage attack on the peace-loving Norwegians. It was a painfully tragic event, and the Japanese people share in the tremendous sorrow of all Norwegians. On behalf of SGI members in

192 countries and territories around the world, I sent messages to Prime Minister Jens Stoltenberg and Foreign Minister Jonas Gahr Støre expressing our deepest condolences.

I was also in contact with SGI members in Norway. They told me that although it was a terribly shocking incident, they renewed their vow to come together for the sake of peace and nonviolence.

REES: Can anything be learned from the brutality in Norway? An answer to this question has come from the dignified Prime Minister Stoltenberg. He has said the best way to resist violence is with more democracy, more openness, and more tolerance and solidarity among peace-loving peoples.

In that respect, every page of our dialogue has echoed that vision and those hopes. I also hope that those who read our conversations will remember the lessons from Norway and will continue to promote nonviolence as the indispensable law for life for all people and in all its forms.

IKEDA: I share your sentiments completely. I believe that the history of the Norwegian people, despite the countless vicissitudes they have experienced, embodies the exceptional qualities of a democratic society, serving as a model we may all follow.

As one indication of this, the media reported in May 2011 an index that ranks countries in terms of the quality of the environment for mothers and children. The index, compiled by the international nongovernmental organization (NGO) Save the Children, covered 164 countries. Norway came first, with Australia in second place. Japan ranked twenty-eighth.[2] The survey also ranked the social conditions for women, and Australia ranked first, Norway second.[3] What better barometer to show a nation's maturity than an index measuring how we care about mothers and children?

Traditionally, when we think about indices that assess the characteristics or performance of various countries, we generally refer to those that measure economic activity, such as Gross Domestic Product and per capita Gross National Income. However, the many virtues of a country and its potential for the future cannot be measured by economic values alone. There is growing interest in indices that focus on human beings, such as the degree to which their dignity is protected and how happy they feel. Examples include the Human Development Index announced by the United Nations Development Programme, and Gross National Happiness, which was proposed by the former king of Bhutan.

In terms of peace and the people's happiness, Norway stands out.

REES: Being the country that came first in the results of the Save the Children survey you mentioned, Norway is always the country that gives me a sense of hope for humanity. The Global Peace Index measures most of the world's countries in terms of their commitment to peace and nonviolence rather than their preparedness for war. Norway is almost always at the top of the rankings. The Norwegians are generous in their contributions to overseas aid, highly supportive of the United Nations and of human rights, and, in their domestic policies, have a strong commitment to equality.

IKEDA: You remind me of discussions I've had with friends proud to have come from Norway. They include the peace scholar Dr. Johan Galtung; Dr. Sverre Lodgaard, the former director of the Peace Research Institute Oslo; and Dr. Elise M. Boulding, the renowned matriarch of the peace studies movement in the United States.

In my dialogue with Dr. Boulding, we talked about the courageous struggle of the Norwegians when their country was invaded by the Nazis during World War II. The Norwegians were united in their nonviolent resistance, establishing an underground communications network and refusing to cooperate with the Nazi occupiers. Even during the war, they made sure to provide their children with peace education.

When I asked Dr. Boulding how Norwegians were able to take such a valiant, enlightened course of action despite the harsh, even life-threatening circumstances they faced, she replied:

> Over the centuries, the Norwegians built up strong regional communities with rules for coping with differences. Although we did not use the words at the time, looking back now, I see that what they were doing was building a peace culture across all the intermountain valleys.[4]

The bonds shared within a community that provide people with mutual sustenance and a sense of safekeeping can inspire immense courage. The solidarity of civil society is vital in building peace.

In 2009, PRIO and the Norwegian Institute of International Affairs joined with the SGI to cosponsor in Oslo our antinuclear weapons exhibition "From a Culture of Violence to a Culture of Peace: Transforming the Human Spirit." At that time, Foreign Minister Støre, while offering kind words for the SGI and its promotion of a grassroots peace movement, observed that "what makes human life unique is the scale of our choice, the degree to which we are free to . . . choose between a culture of violence or a culture of peace."[5] This time-honored, sublime spirit of peace thrives in Norway to this day.

By the way, how did you and your wife meet?

## A HEALTHY CIVIL SOCIETY

REES: I first saw Ragnhild on Platform 13 of London's Kings Cross Station. She had just arrived from Norway; I was on my way to Cambridge for the weekend and by chance had decided that I might be able to get a train from Kings Cross. I had just returned from a couple months as a student in the Soviet Union and was already in high spirits when I noticed this beautiful young woman on the station platform talking to other young men. I asked if I could help her! Subsequently, on a journey on the London Underground, I obtained her name and arranged to meet her a week later on the steps of the church of St. Martin-in-the-Fields in Trafalgar Square.

Our friendship grew, and about eighteen months later we married in Norway, in the middle of a very snowy winter. It was a year of heavy snowfalls. To even begin the drive to the ancient church, we had to dig large snowdrifts away from her parents' home.

Our life together has involved a series of adventures, but those adventures—in several different countries—have been made possible because Ragnhild is the great homemaker, adapts skillfully to new demands, and has that firm but gentle demeanor that provides for a usually calm atmosphere, even with a husband who deals with and sometimes creates conflicts. Our adventures have taken us to work in London, in Scotland, in Canada, several times in the United States, and for more than three decades in Australia.

Ragnhild's selflessness enabled me to build a career, to spend endless hours writing books, and to work and travel in countries such as India and Sri Lanka, while she maintained our home, cared for our children, was a generous host to others, and developed her own career teaching crafts of various kinds, always to the highest possible standards. In that respect, she's a perfectionist. She is also an imaginative and skilled cook, whereas my cooking skills are very limited.

IKEDA: I am very much aware that Ragnhild is an amazing woman. When I met you both in April 2009, I was struck by her smile, which was as gentle and comforting as a spring breeze.

REES: I have met your wife, Kaneko, in Singapore and in Tokyo. Her warmth and hospitality gave me an immediate sense of being at ease. Her commitment to peace with justice and her support for you must have been indispensable. It has always been empowering to be with your wife, even if I could not express those sentiments in Japanese.

IKEDA: Thank you very much for your kind words. Kaneko will be delighted. We both treasure wonderful memories of the times we spent with you.

I suffered from tuberculosis and other ailments when I was young, and my doctor said I would not live to thirty. Despite my fragile health, it was my wife who enabled me to carry out activities for peace—travelling throughout Japan and the world, meeting with countless people. I owe it to her extensive care and support.

Given my hectic schedule during my visits overseas, Kaneko served at times as my nurse and at other times as my nutritionist, paying the utmost attention to my meals and health. She is my kindred spirit—my closest comrade-in-arms—absolutely irreplaceable.

I once wrote her this poem as an expression of my undying gratitude:

> The path opens;
> I step forward, together with you,
> my inseparable support.

REES: I understand the strong union between your wife and yourself, and I can see how significant that is, in both your lives. I, too, have great respect for my wife: for her selflessness, her gentle charm, and her considerable tolerance of me, of demanding children, and of any of life's difficulties.

In my middle thirties, I experienced several months of depression. It was the reactive kind, but I did experience feelings of powerlessness and lack of self-worth that made me pessimistic and fatalistic. There's no doubt that what helped me to recover were the love and support of my wife, the realization that I was dragging her down, too, and the understanding that this was unfair. We also took a break and went overseas for several months. The change of context, culture, and climate also helped my recovery.

IKEDA: I see that you and your wife have experienced life's changing seasons and overcome them through your love and support for each other. Such golden experiences help brighten and encourage many people's lives.

Nichiren encourages a wife and husband to "work together like the sun and moon, a pair of eyes, or the two wings of a bird"[6] and lead their lives with hearts united. He also writes, "It is the power of the bow that determines the flight of the arrow . . . and the strength of the wife that guides the actions of her husband."[7] This suggests the central role of women both in society and the family. Over the years, I have met many prominent individuals around the world, leaders in various fields of endeavor, and with the great men I have met, there have always been great women standing alongside.

The former president of the Soviet Union, Mikhail Gorbachev, and his brilliant partner, Raisa, were both passionate about the most sublime aspirations, choosing to ascend together the steepest peaks to improve society. Mr. Gorbachev once said that *perestroika* itself would have been impossible without her.

I will never forget Raisa, a few years after her husband resigned from the presidency, telling me:

> Somehow, we made it through the past few years. I some-times wonder how we managed to do so. We had such a struggle just to survive. . . . My husband experienced much suffering and betrayal, but he has continued to fight for the sake of the whole world. I, who have been at his side throughout, can attest that he was never fighting for his own interests.

Sadly, Raisa died from an illness. Several years have passed, but the memories my wife and I have of meeting her remain golden.

There is much to be learned from remarkable relationships between husbands and wives. Are there other couples who have left a deep impression on you?

REES: Well, if I can give the names of a couple who have been very close to me—the late Pat Toms and her husband, Bruce, who made a significant contribution to Australia's civil society. Former schoolteachers, they also spent twenty years as invaluable orga-nizers of Sydney's weekly public forum known as "Politics in the Pub."

Despite Pat's frail health and Bruce's advanced age, they con-tinued to be a source of ideas about social justice and the poli-tics of social change, and were unfailing in their attendance at the weekly forums. They were generous, humorous, and enabling people. They were also the main creators, editors, and distributors of a social justice magazine called *Australian Socialist*.

IKEDA: They sound like a splendid couple who found joyful pur-pose in working for society. They serve as a fine example of citi-zens' community activism, which is democracy's foundation.

Thinking of their collaborative publishing venture, I am reminded of Mahatma Gandhi's second son, Manilal, and his wife, Sushila, who took over publication of the *Indian Opinion,* a newspaper launched by Gandhi in South Africa. Sushila Gandhi's hearing became impaired as a side effect of a malaria treatment. When she immigrated to South Africa, she could not speak any English, yet she mastered the language through sheer effort. She threw herself into helping out with the newspaper's typesetting and mastered Gujarati, the language of the western part of India, to the point where she could write columns in the language.

Both husband and wife continued to wholeheartedly oppose racial inequality in South Africa. Their son, Arun Gandhi, once shared with me his recollection of that time:

> I myself helped with the printing of the newspaper from the age of about ten. In those days, typesetting was carried out by hand, and we printed manually one page at a time.
>
> But my father had two greater problems. The first was oppression from the government, which tried to censor the content of the columns. Father would never comply. The second problem was shortage of money. There was nobody to help with publication of the newspaper, and my father struggled to obtain funds.
>
> I, too, walked around encouraging people to take the newspaper, and I was spoken to in such a humiliating way: "I've never heard of or read such a newspaper." "If you're in difficulty, I'll buy a copy. But I won't read it."
>
> I used to complain to my father and tell him these experiences, and he would encourage me, saying: "Don't worry. For every unkind person, there are ten who are kind. So don't worry about unkind ones. Just look at the kind people."

I find the adamantine belief and stirring confidence in human-ity that underlie his father's insights to be extraordinary and enriching.

When Arun Gandhi told me this story, I responded:

> If at that time, your father had instead joined you in anger or sadness, then the two of you might have slid toward failure. With these few words, your father guided both of you toward the path to victory, didn't he?

Mr. Gandhi nodded in deep agreement.

REES: When a child is faced with a problem or is about to give up, it is very important for a father to know how to handle the situation.

We have three children—two daughters and one son. They were born in different countries and for a time travelled on different passports: Canadian, British, and Australian. Love was the central ingredient in bringing up our children, but this never meant allowing just any kind of behavior. Our philosophy was and is that if you care for someone, then it's appropriate and responsible to intervene, to gently but firmly stress the values that you hold and that you want them to live by.

Giving our children opportunities in every possible sphere of life was also a guiding principle, for the simple reason that this made life more interesting, as long as they never pursued their own interests at the expense of other people. Our children were taken on camping holidays, were given opportunities in sports and music, and were encouraged in every aspect of their education.

Our eldest daughter, Heidi—born in the Canadian Rockies—is a speech therapist. She is married with two children and lives with her husband, an attorney, in Melbourne. Our second daughter, Tania—born in Scotland—manages a music publishing company.

She studied music at Queensland Conservatorium, where she met her husband, a very accomplished clarinet player with the Sydney Symphony Orchestra. They have two children and live in Sydney. Our son was born in Sydney and, in many ways, is a typical sports-loving Australian. He obtained his doctorate in sports science and teaches at the Australian Institute of Sport. He lives with his girl-friend in inner-city Sydney.

IKEDA: When your family gets together, it must be like a school for studying cultural diversity.

It is vital for parents to instill in their children basic human values, just as you and your wife have done. In the long run, a life without a sense of purpose and responsibility will inevitably be unstable, like a house with no pillars. It is impossible to lead a life of fulfillment and satisfaction without a framework of stalwart character.

With this in mind, I have always taught children the impor-tance of acquainting themselves with good books. The British statesman John Bright once said: "What is a great love of books? It is something like a personal introduction to the great and good men of all past times."[8]

Those who encounter great individuals of all ages and cultures, and learn inspiration time after time through books read in their youth are blessed. To be introduced to men and women of excep-tional character and vision broadens the vistas of the reader's life and nourishes his or her soul; it becomes a major force for self-development.

REES: In a house full of books and with visitors who were chal-lenging and interesting, my children learned the value of study and how to persist in spite of the temptation to give up. The pres-ence of books in the home and the regular raising of questions about current affairs probably contributed to an atmosphere in

which it was obvious that education was valued. As a father, I'm
sure I always insisted that progress in life was impossible without
the benefits of education.

I was a believer in teasing in order to identify a young person's
characteristics. Their mother was kinder, probably more tolerant,
and certainly the person who showed by example the values of
consistency and caring in the home. I also emphasized the value
of public-sector services in tandem with individual effort. Public
schooling, public health, and social (public) welfare have an effect
on family life because these services provide the means to build
a civil society.

IKEDA: A healthy civil society can be said to exist when self-help
(the individual), mutual-help (support for one another), and
public-help (support by the public sector) are all present. These
pluralistic supports are essential in constructing a safe, anxiety-
free society, as we have witnessed in the wake of the Great East
Japan Earthquake.

In the field of education, it is imperative to respect each child
as an individual personality. Within the heart of a child, there is an
adult, and we should address this individual with sincere respect.

Apparently, when Arun Gandhi was about ten, he was the
victim of a physical attack inspired by racial prejudice in South
Africa. Unable to control his indignation, he yearned to grow up
as soon as possible, to become strong enough to humiliate any
assailant, regardless of who that might be, with brute force. It was
then that his parents sent him to India to be cared for by his grandfather. After listening to his grandson, Gandhi told him that if
anything made him angry, he should write his feelings down in
a journal, describing the way he felt every time his anger threatened to consume him. We often let our emotions spill out, doing
and saying things that are hurtful toward others, Gandhi said, but

pouring his anger out on the journal pages enabled him to let it go and discover constructive solutions.

Arun Gandhi took his grandfather's words to heart and strove to ensure that his mind was not ruled by anger, and that he would use the energy generated by his anger to seek positive solutions. A passage from Nichiren's writings maintains that anger can be a function of either good or evil.[9] If we stand with high purpose and a moral sense, even the energy generated from anger can lead to actions for peace and justice, and actions of nonviolence. This is evidence of the profound mission of humanistic education.

REES: In several jobs in different countries, I have always encouraged students, friends, and colleagues to record and reflect on the ways they handle conflicts. Such recording and reflecting have been valuable in learning the language of nonviolence. As with any language, we have to practice. The conduct of relationships in any context—in family, in work, and in faith-based, political, or voluntary organizations—provides opportunities to practice nonviolence.

The essence of nonviolence is expressed through those words, in any language, that express identity, love, justice, beauty, affection, and peace. Nonviolence is also expressed through art, music, poetry, with the clothes we wear, the food we eat, the way we decorate and furnish our homes, and the hospitality we show to others. Expressions of hospitality and gratitude for hospitality can be made on an almost daily basis.

I have always valued my friendship with SGI members on account of their generous hospitality, as well as their promotion of music and art. When I visited Japan, I had the opportunity to listen to the musicians at the Min-On Culture Center. It was an encouraging and much appreciated experience. I was inspired to write a haiku to remind me of the occasion:

Music is the cure,
love provides the notes
for all the people's hopes.

Silence is a language,
nonviolence the currency,
poetry the means of exchange.

I notice that I referred to *love* in this poem. I suspect that love for a common humanity—not just for those with whom we are intimate—characterizes inspiring plays, wonderful music, photographs, painting, or poetry.

IKEDA: I agree. It is important to strengthen our grasp of the language of nonviolence and express the principles of nonviolence in a variety of ways in our daily lives and relationships.

All the great religions teach that every human being possesses unlimited potential and extraordinary strength. And fine poems, art, and music have the power to enrich the human heart, elevate one's dignity, and unite people.

As I explained earlier (see Conversation One), Makiguchi and Toda, inspired by the peace philosophy of Buddhism, opposed Japanese militarism through the nonviolent means of speech and dialogue. Even imprisonment could not defeat them. Under harsh interrogation in prison, they cried out for justice to the very end and never compromised their beliefs. This history is the proud starting point of our SGI peace movement.

In 1975, I summed this up:

Various powers in the world—authority, brutality and money—attempt to violate human dignity. The role of the Soka Gakkai in society is to employ the spirit that wells from the very depths of life to do battle with such powers.[10]

This is the core of the "human revolution"[11] movement that we of the SGI promote.

I am reminded of these words by the French author André Maurois: "The more profound revolutions are spiritual. They transform people, who in turn transform the world."[12] Maurois was a firm advocate of the need to create a society that treasures the happiness of mothers and children, which we discussed earlier.

Efforts to realize "peace with justice," which is the central theme of our dialogue, depend as much upon this kind of inner transformation as on the actions we take in society. It is only through the ceaseless interplay between these internal and external efforts that we can achieve our aim.

CONVERSATION SIX

# Unsung Heroes

IKEDA: There is an Eastern maxim that Makiguchi treasured: "From the indigo, an even deeper blue."[1] This refers to the fact that, although blue dye comes from the indigo plant, when a fabric is dyed repeatedly, its color becomes even bluer than that of the indigo plant itself. This maxim expresses a desire for future generations to surpass their seniors and grow into fine human beings.

Makiguchi urged teachers to become good companions of the children they teach, supporting their growth. "The ideal teacher," he declared as he pioneered a path to true humanistic education, "is one who stands on the principle of rendering guidance that will lead pupils to the highest level of character, enabling them to surpass even the teacher."[2]

When I was young, Toda would tell us youth:

There is a saying in *The Analects of Confucius* that we must regard the next generation with "awe," for there is no knowing how much they may grow. You are the next generation, so it is your job to achieve more than I have.

He said this to challenge us, out of his desire to see us grow. I, too, have focused my energy on nurturing young people for the same reason.

REES: There is no greater joy for an educator than watching his or her former students achieving personal growth and development. I do value the observations of past students that my classes were inspiring, and that my support for their research enabled them to complete their theses to their satisfaction and to a high standard.

Although I still value close relationships with students at the university level, there are two trends that hinder such closeness and even discourage a passion for learning. The first trend concerns the increasing costs of higher education and the financial difficulties faced by students even if they want to study full time.

The second trend concerns students' reliance on all the machinery—including iPads, iPhones—of the computer age. Such reliance should not replace the informality and the dialogue that characterize more traditional means of education. I shall remember students whose commitments and company I have enjoyed. I doubt that I'll ever remember someone who only communicated with me electronically.

IKEDA: A diamond can only be polished by another diamond. Likewise, human beings must be forged among other human beings to shine even brighter. I want to see students learning freely in an environment that is inspirational and encourages heart-to-heart exchange. Nothing makes me happier than to see the vibrant, unhindered development of young people.

Soka University of America reached a milestone in 2011 with its tenth anniversary; it held its seventh graduation ceremony that May and welcomed the Class of 2015 that August. They are all excellent students who could have gone to prestigious universities in their own countries if they had wished. Instead, they came to study at the university I established. I will be praying that they all lead lives of great growth, achievement, and success. My concern and expectations for them will remain for the rest of my life.

I was pleased to see that *Newsweek* magazine in 2010 ranked SUA among the top 25 of 3,000 universities throughout the United States in four categories, including "Most Desirable Small Schools" and "Most Diverse Schools."[3] We place the highest priority on our students, devoting the utmost attention to honor and enrich the individuality and character of everyone in our care. This is the tradition of humanistic education established at SUA, and I am profoundly delighted, as founder, by the *Newsweek* recognition.

REES: From my experience teaching at various universities throughout the world, I'd say as a generalization that where classes in certain universities in the United States were large, students were often fed facts to be subsequently tested in examinations. This is an unfortunate rote learning style, which could be as boring as it is unimaginative. Of course, this is different from the principle of small classes promoted by SUA.

In Canada and the United Kingdom, the European tradition of expecting students to be largely self-taught encouraged learning habits that could last a lifetime. In such a context, the teacher's role was to motivate and inspire students rather than prepare them for tests.

IKEDA: You raise an important point. As you have done yourself, I think it is essential to discover ways to encourage students to take the initiative and enable them to display their talent. It is also important that youth have plenty of opportunities to be exposed to great works of literature and art.

I am reminded of a discussion I had with the former prime minister of Thailand, Anand Panyarachun, in October 2000. When the conversation turned to education that cultivates creativity, the former prime minister stressed that it is essential to connect children with great literature, art, culture, and people, enabling children to experience quality in every aspect of life. Mr. Anand's view resonates with those of us who uphold the tradition of Soka education, as it is precisely what we have consistently worked to achieve ourselves.

In May 2011, we completed the Soka Performing Arts Center at SUA to add to an educational environment that fosters creativity. In many universities around the world that I have visited over the years, such cultural facilities serve as centers for sharing art and peace with a broad audience; they also serve as arenas in which local citizens can engage in meaningful exchange. We at the Soka universities hope to learn from those universities with time-honored histories as we strive to provide a highly creative education, one enabling the arts and culture to flower to the fullest.

REES: Many congratulations on the opening of the Soka Performing Arts Center. The University of Sydney's cultural facilities, such as the Nicholson Museum and the War Memorial Art Gallery, are attractive to a wide public of tourists, schoolchildren's tours, and specialist students and staff.

By "specialist," I'm referring to those students who are studying antiquities, archaeology, ancient history, and the history of art. The very existence of these facilities on the university campus gives that cosmopolitan flavor that characterizes the notion of university—open to all ideas, giving great respect to history, providing opportunities to view great art and learn from it.

IKEDA: It is an outstanding endeavor by the University of Sydney. I agree that when a university provides the opportunity for people to encounter and be enlightened by various cultures and the arts, it can truly be called a pantheon where human wisdom and creativity will shine without limit.

At the center of the coat of arms of the University of Sydney is an open book. I have felt that it symbolizes an institution where world citizens learn with an open mind. The Tokyo Fuji Art Museum was established on a site adjacent to Soka University in Tokyo for similar reasons, in the hopes it would serve society.

I'd also like to mention that the SUA alumni—the men and women who, since the first graduating class, have taken great pride in their alma mater as young cofounders—are proving to be of service in many walks of life, forging new paths where none existed before. Aware that they are blazing new trails for the sake of SUA students who will follow them, many of our graduates have been accepted into the postgraduate programs of universities throughout the world, including Harvard, Stanford, and Columbia, as well as Cambridge, Oxford, and other prestigious institutions around the world.

In your experience, what do graduates need to bear in mind when continuing their research after graduation? I would appreciate hearing your opinion about this based on your own involvement in postgraduate education over many years.

REES: I am delighted to answer that question. I have supervised hundreds of masters and doctoral students. I'm mostly concerned about what they believe in, what they stand for, and what they want to do with their lives. Teaching them about research, how to write and analyze, is made possible if these more personal issues are also addressed. I try to establish relationships based on friendship as well as on intellectual challenge.

I also insist that students attain the highest possible standards of research and writing. I encourage students to take a stand on social issues, to "walk the walk," as well as "talk the talk." Such involvement in social action is a way of leading by example and is a valuable means of student learning.

In these respects, the mentor role can be played in many ways. As indicated by my relationship with my Scottish professor-supervisor Raymond Illsley, whom I mentioned earlier (see Conversations Two and Three), the mentor-student relationship is a great way to learn.

IKEDA: In advancing along the path of scholarship, students will be directionless without a reliable compass in life that reminds them of the key question, "For what purpose?" (see Conversation Two). In other words, I believe it is essential, for the rest of our lives, to ponder how best to live as a human being—this is vital if we are to continue learning with a humble attitude and further our growth, as we return to basic principles.

In May 2010, we welcomed to Soka University of Japan a delegation from the prestigious Université Laval, of which Canada is justly proud. Established in 1663, it is the oldest French-language university in North America. Rector Denis Brière emphasized that the key to a victorious life in this tumultuous age of constant change lies above all in continuing to learn for a lifetime.

The university's Faculty of Educational Sciences has a distinguished history and tradition, and is now seeking to develop a new graduate degree in planetary citizenship. We were honored to learn that Dr. Brière has paid close attention to Soka education principles in setting this up.

Under a new academic initiative to promote global citizenship, Soka University of Japan and SUA have organized special courses and lecture presentations, inviting leaders and intellectuals active in many fields throughout the world as lecturers. In April 2011, the historian Vincent Harding, a close friend of Martin Luther King Jr., participated in "A Conversation on How to Educate for Nonviolent Citizenship," an SUA panel discussion. This is one of the themes I examined with Dr. Harding in our dialogue, *America Will Be!: Conversations on Hope, Freedom, and Democracy.*

Discussing what contributed to the success of such civil rights battles as the Montgomery bus boycott, led by Dr. King, Dr. Harding stated:

> We do a disservice to the whole idea of a people's movement if we attribute a movement's success or failure to the efforts of one charismatic leader. King was inspired by the people, and he inspired them as well. It was a constant give-and-take relationship.[4]

Having said that, he underscored the following point:

> It is undeniable that the success of this movement originated in the determination, courage, and endurance of the people. They continued to refuse to use the city bus system for an entire year. Most of the people who depended on the buses were ordinary working-class people—maids, cooks, janitors, and porters. . . . Ordinary people acted with courage, they saw one another acting courageously, and this was another reason for the success of the boycott. . . .
>
> They were determined to walk rather than be insulted any longer.[5]

## WHAT MAKES A HERO

REES: It is a story that makes us ponder deeply. I have the same belief myself, that inspiring people exist among the humblest of citizens, even if they are not well known.

Therefore, I was cautious and a little critical of the seminar "What Makes a Champion?," which featured outstanding figures from various fields, coinciding with the Sydney Olympic Games in

September 2000. Even though this event was partially instrumental in bringing President Nelson Mandela to Australia, I felt there was something in the way the conference was held that jarred with my longstanding conviction.

Actually, there are many people around me who could be called "unsung heroes and heroines." Typical of such people are Pat and Bruce Toms, the couple whom I previously introduced (see Conversation Five) and who organized Sydney's weekly public forum known as "Politics in the Pub." Although not well known, they made a significant contribution to Australia's civil society.

Perhaps another unsung hero is my colleague Hannah Middleton, who is the executive officer of the Sydney Peace Foundation. Despite a life-threatening illness, Hannah, together with her husband, Denis Doherty, is selfless in her work for social justice and in her leadership of protests against injustice. Coupled with her cherished values of support for nonviolence and for demilitarization, her humor and political skills are also invaluable features of her life and work.

IKEDA: I am impressed by your insight in discovering true champions from among common citizens. Those extolled as champions of humanity or heroes of peace—like King and Mandela, who imparted courage and hope and played central roles in transforming history—are by no means the only ones who can serve as models of inspiration worthy of emulation. I agree with you that we should direct our attention to the nameless ordinary people whose lives shine as they firmly strive to live in a praiseworthy way.

The contrast is reminiscent of the differing views of the philosophers Thomas Carlyle and Ralph Waldo Emerson on what makes a hero. Carlyle contended that the heroic figure has special abilities different from those of ordinary people, whereas Emerson considered all people to be innately endowed with greatness and able to develop this potential and bring it to full flower. Emerson once said, "I remember how many obscure persons I myself have seen possessing gifts that excited wonder, speculation and delight in me. . . ."[6] He made it clear that he admired and treasured such people, even though society would never bestow on them the recognition they warranted. Looking back on my own life, I feel that these words by Emerson resonate deeply with the truth.

REES: Emerson's view of heroes and humankind that you have introduced overlaps my own beliefs. In fact, these unsung heroes are the very foundation in building a peaceful world. And when we investigate why and how peace persists in post-conflict societies, we usually discover that humble but courageous and skilled women are the key figures in such achievements.

IKEDA: I have consistently advocated that women hold the key to building peace. They may not generate much fanfare, but women—as well as other unidentified citizens—working to build a more peaceful society are indispensable to advancing peace.

It's been more than thirty years since I published *Wasureenu deai* (Unforgettable Encounters), a compilation of magazine essays I wrote about my treasured memories of ordinary people whom I encountered in my youth. It also featured world-renowned intellectuals with whom I conducted dialogues, such as Toynbee and Aurelio Peccei, Club of Rome cofounder.

As one example, when I was in elementary school, I delivered newspapers, and there was a young couple in the neighborhood who encouraged and always cared about me. They would say: "You know of Edison, the great inventor. He was a paperboy when he was in school, too. People who experience hardship when they are young are truly fortunate."

There was also Yumichi Takata, principal of the night school I attended after the war. A passionate educator, he put all his might into nurturing us youth who were studying while working, initially commuting from a hospital, where he was undergoing treatment, to the school, which he had opened. Later, he took up lodgings in the school and worked from there. Takata strove to overcome his illness and convert his school into a college, surviving long enough to see the college established.

And there was Takeo Kurobe, the owner of the printing company I worked at in those days. He put up with all manner of hardship, working hard round the clock. Yet, every day at closing time, he always went out of his way to send me off to my evening classes.

I introduced my recollections of many other ordinary people in the series. As I wrote, "There is an unfailing brilliancy of character among the ordinary people who constantly strive to be true to themselves."[7]

In addition, there are countless SGI members who, while their names may never be recognized, have led lives of greatness and stellar nobility, working with me over the years in the struggle to establish a "century of peace and human dignity." I began writing essays about these SGI members in 1980 to honor their precious lives and to commit their memory to posterity. Eventually, I introduced more than 100 of these "unforgettable SGI comrades" in the *Seikyo Shimbun* series. I have also depicted the dramatic lives of tens of thousands of champions among the people in other essays and in my serialized novels, *The Human Revolution* and *The New Human Revolution*.

REES: It is an extremely significant undertaking. In my book *Achieving Power: Practice and Policy in Social Welfare*, I introduced my notion of the "promise of biography," a concept that describes the potential creativity that lies within all human beings. Too often, however, and for reasons of gender or racial discrimination, lack of self-worth or lack of basic educational opportunities, that promise is not realized. An essential feature of future social activities could be to focus on the "promise of biography," especially the stories of those who seldom feature in our usual participation in music, art, humanist politics, and related activities.

Having said that, I admit to being impressed when SGI members have had an opportunity to explain their stories in public and, in that way, gain self-confidence and understanding.

IKEDA: I appreciate your acknowledgment. The Lotus Sutra, which many consider to represent the essence of Mahayana Buddhism, contains the phrases "various causes and conditions" and "various similes and parables." They indicate that Shakyamuni Buddha utilized an array of causal associations and metaphors to explain difficult Buddhist principles in concrete, readily understandable terms.

Toda would often point out that the example of a human being who has overcome adversity is the greatest source of encouragement to people facing the same problems. Whether it is the suffering one experiences from sickness, a problem in the family or with work, or the sorrow of losing someone close, unless we have experienced similar suffering ourselves, it is difficult to understand the pain of those in distress. Toda once said:

> Why was I able to become the president of the Soka Gakkai? The reason is that I lost my wife. I lost my beloved daughter. And I have tasted life's bitter hardships to the hilt. That is why I was able to become the president.[8]

Prevailing over hardship after hardship through faith proves one's triumph as an individual, offering those suffering from similar problems a glimmer of hope and courage. It is a process of transforming personal adversity into the kindling to illuminate other people's lives. SGI members have supported one another in living based on this spirit, in which we strive for the happiness of ourselves as well as others.

I once wrote the following lyrics describing our resolve to transform the ordeals that we have undergone into a lifelong commitment to lighting the flame of courage in others' hearts:

Forge ahead, and I will forge ahead, too,
pressing on through blizzards, we boldly advance.
If we are truly Bodhisattvas of the Earth,
then we have a mission to fulfill in this world.[9]

REES: I interpret these words to mean that the stamina and perseverance of people who carry heavy burdens lie at the heart of humanity, and that such examples of "pressing on through blizzards" should encourage those of us who have been more fortunate in life.

I have in my mind the pictures of women from Somalia who have walked for many days and often for weeks with their malnourished children to try to find help and refuge in refugee camps in Kenya. In spite of the most extreme conditions, walking with no food and little water, they have shown such courage and dignity. Let us hope that although many Somalian children and mothers have died, UN intervention will prevent a humanitarian catastrophe.

IKEDA: I totally agree. Nothing moves us more than to see individuals rise above the most unforgiving circumstances, even life-or-death situations, to safeguard their beloved families, to reach out and help their friends.

Despite experiencing their own grief and difficulties as a result of the Great East Japan Earthquake, many Soka Gakkai members have devoted themselves to working with others to encourage and assist fellow residents in stricken communities, extending the circle of solace and sustenance far beyond their own lives. As you stated, the admirable service rendered by such people has touched countless Japanese citizens, imparting courage and hope.

The morning after the calamity, one Soka Gakkai member in Kamaishi, Iwate Prefecture, began working with people of the local neighborhood association and the fire brigade to rescue a small village that had been cut off from surrounding communities due to the flooding caused by the tsunami. Over the next three days, they removed rubble across a two-and-a-half-mile stretch of land to create a "lifeline." They even built a temporary heliport.

"I love this town and its people," the man explained. "I wanted to save them. Everybody worked with one another and became totally absorbed in the rescue effort."

Others have offered similar testimony, noting that the compelling desire to help and be of service to other people enabled them to draw forth immense inner strength. Young people have also risen to the challenge in communities throughout the stricken areas, their selfless contributions continuing to this day. Indeed, the vitality and passion of young people who embrace their own purpose and meaning in life are sources of hope for a new era. No matter how deep the darkness, dawn will invariably arrive wherever youth stand tall.

REES: Related to this, you emphasized the "role of youth in challenging seemingly intractable social realities and creating a new era" in your annual peace proposal in January 2011.[10] Recently, we have witnessed educated and courageous youth rising and taking action in Middle Eastern countries, such as Tunisia and Egypt. Although they may have come from different family and educational backgrounds, the youth stood up to protect democracy and human rights, and achieved a significant victory through the means of nonviolence. These young people from the Middle East seized an opportunity.

All around the world, all youth might also insist on the elimination of nuclear weapons of all kinds. Such elimination—a nuclear-free world—is essential for the construction of a society where universal human rights are respected. If young people commit themselves to a nuclear-free world, the future of humankind will surely be much brighter.

Courage is required in the struggle of nonviolence. On the contrary, to threaten others and use violence to threaten them are acts of cowardice. I think your advocacy of urging people, in particular youth, to put such nonviolent ideas into practice finds resonance with Mahatma Gandhi's conviction that nonviolence is a law for life.

CONVERSATION SEVEN

# A World Without Nuclear Weapons

IKEDA: November 2011 marked the centenary of the departure from Sydney Harbor of a Japanese ship led by Lieutenant Nobu Shirase on a pioneering voyage to the Antarctic.

Shirase once stated:

> Adversity and obstacles are bound to arise when we set out to accomplish anything. Success achieved without difficulty is not true success but sheer luck. Such success is like winning a lottery.[1]

Shirase came from Akita Prefecture in northeastern Japan. He embarked on the challenge to explore the Antarctic, leading a party from Japan at the time when Roald Amundsen and Robert Scott were engaged in a fierce, famous race to be first to the South Pole. The Shirase party had previously embarked on an Antarctic landing in February 1911 but found itself icebound and forced to turn back in disappointment. They remained in Sydney until the ice melted, whereupon they made another attempt.

In those days, the Japanese were often treated with prejudice and suspicion in Sydney. When the party arrived in Sydney, the local newspapers were filled with caustic accounts regarding them with suspicion.

The man who had the courage to stand up in support of the Japanese party at that time was the famous geologist and explorer Sir Edgeworth David, then a professor at the University of Sydney. David, who had experienced Antarctic exploration himself, visited the members of the Shirase party soon after they arrived. In addition to encouraging them personally, he praised their attempt in a statement published in the newspapers, insisting that the local community had a duty to support the expedition from Japan.

From that time on, the mood among Sydney residents improved dramatically, and many extended the expedition members a warm welcome. For the rest of their stay in Australia, local hospitality was lavished on the Japanese party. Looking back on that time with gratitude, Shirase fondly described Sydney as his "hometown for half a year."[2]

REES: I am delighted to know that a hundred years ago, a professor from the University of Sydney played a pioneering role in correcting people's perception of the Japanese, and that Lieutenant Shirase deepened his affection so far as to call Sydney his hometown. I am also impressed by the "Shirase principle," that to obtain success, you usually have to overcome various obstacles, including hardships.

IKEDA: Once it reached Sydney Harbor, the Japanese party was on its own for some time, so Professor David was surely a source of tremendous support. In addition to data about Antarctica, he provided a great deal of valuable advice and information. In the expedition record that Shirase wrote on his return to Japan, he noted on numerous occasions the expedition's debt of gratitude to the professor, and that his assistance proved indispensable.

On November 19, 1911, when the party once again set out from

Sydney Harbor for Antarctica, Professor David visited the expedition ship so that he could see them off until the last minute. Shirase later said that it would take a very long time before he would forget the sight of the grey-haired professor who, despite his advanced age, went to such great lengths to send them off.[3]

By way of bidding farewell to the professor, Shirase presented him with a Japanese sword that he had treasured, a gesture of his deep, abiding gratitude and respect. That sword is now in the Australian Museum in Sydney but was returned to Japan from July–August 2011 for a special exhibition in commemoration of the 150th anniversary of Shirase's birth. The exhibition attracted considerable attention as a symbol of the profound, exquisite friendship struck between these forefathers of our two countries.

REES: At this time of such divisive politics around the world, and as I think of the tragedy of so many young people murdered in my wife's home country, Norway, in July 2011, as we discussed earlier (see Conversation Five), that reference to a bond between two peoples is so encouraging. Expressions of solidarity among people, even if they do not share a common language, can do so much to promote understanding and a shared purpose. Even the emotional expression of solidarity can be regarded as a common language. We all benefit from such solidarity, as in our shared lifelong commitment, yours and mine, to universal human rights and to nonviolence, including striving for a nuclear-free world.

## AN HONEST VIEW OF HISTORY

IKEDA: Solidarity for peace should be the world's rallying cry in the twenty-first century. Unfortunately, Japan grew more belligerent as it plummeted along the path of militarism in the early twentieth century. Then, in World War II, Japan carried out bombing raids as far away as your beautiful country, notably the City of Darwin, taking many precious lives. It was absolutely deplorable.

The first two Soka Gakkai presidents fought against militarism without compromise. I and my fellow Soka Gakkai members are the successors to that spirit, as we work together with those who share this spirit for peace to ensure that war, which exacts the harshest toll on ordinary citizens, never happens again.

The specter of a Japanese invasion must have had an incalculable impact on Australia, especially as she had never faced a threat of that magnitude before. There must surely be many Australians who continue to bear deep wounds from that tragic time in history.

REES: Australians' image of Japan varies according to age. The older generation, who have memories of World War II and of the atrocities committed in prisoner-of-war camps, might still see sadistic features in the Japanese character. They would perhaps recall the Japanese government's reluctance to apologize for atrocities and inhumane conduct in China, the Korean Peninsula, and other countries during World War II.

How we look at the history of our own country and how we learn its lessons are major challenges for any country, and Australia is no exception. Debate about Australia's history continues, usually in the form of the following questions: What was the extent of violence toward Aboriginal people? What was the extent of discrimination against non-Anglo-Saxon ethnic groups? In what ways has Australia benefitted from the arrival of new migrants?

At least the debates about Australia's history are now in the open. The Australian lesson is that there is no point in concealing history, in trying to sanitize events. A vibrant democracy depends on open debate and on courageous admission of the negative sides of history as well as the positive.

IKEDA: It's an extremely important point that you raise. To face the future is impossible without an honest appraisal and proper acknowledgment of the past. Motivated by this belief, I have taken every opportunity to stress to young people how important it is to learn the lessons of history while developing judicious insight and an incisive understanding of the past. In holding dialogues with leaders and intellectuals from other Asian countries, I have consistently striven to bring historical truths into the open to deepen rapport and facilitate mutual understanding.

When I began a dialogue with Dr. Cho Moon-Boo, former president of Jeju National University of South Korea, I expressed my firm resolve:

> Erroneous perceptions of historical events are still deeply ingrained and smoldering. That is why we must resolutely promote peace education based on a correct and honest view of history that transcends such misperceptions, both qualitatively and quantitatively. It is my heartfelt desire that our dialogue will become the cornerstone of that process.[4]

One lesson I have learned from the study of history is the importance of carefully understanding the other party's perspective. This is a point I emphasized in my dialogue with Dr. Zhang Kaiyuan, a leading Chinese historian, which was published in 2010. Dr. Zhang shared his profound insight on this point, saying it is possible to seek and master the truth only through dialogue in which we assume the other's viewpoint, which may vary widely from our own, and try to think like them.[5] His words have stayed with me.

How do other Australians see the Japanese people today?

REES: Well, the younger generation in Australia has different perceptions of Japan. Their image comes from the reputation of the electronic companies or the reputation for reliability of Japanese-manufactured cars.

I have visited Japan several times and realized I was in a country that prided itself on tidiness and efficiency. In addition, I cannot forget the kindheartedness and graciousness shown to me by ordinary citizens during my stays.

I first visited Japan in 1998 and have returned on several occasions. My first visit was to participate in an international social welfare conference. I lodged in an area of Tokyo that had no English-language signs, and for a few days, travel on the railways was challenging: I could not speak any Japanese. However, with the exception of rather stern railway officials, people were overwhelmingly helpful and hospitable. They made a great effort to understand my requests.

In Australia's northwest, in the town of Broome, many Australians retain memories of the skills and bravery of Japanese pearl divers.[6] In that respect, there remains a considerable sense of solidarity between Australians in the northwest of the country—around Broome—and those adventurous, brave Japanese citizens. Among many Australians, that image survives.

IKEDA: These Japanese divers played a pioneering role in broadening friendship between the two countries through exchanges among citizens. Many Japanese moved to Australia in order to collect mother-of-pearl shells, used for expensive buttons for upmarket apparel. It is a matter of record that, from the end of the nineteenth century to the early years of the twentieth, they were engaged in dangerous work in Broome and on Thursday Island, as well as in Darwin.

In addition to mother-of-pearl, wool was one of the oldest products to bind Australia and Japan together. Woolen textile production, which was one of Japan's biggest industries before World War II, was largely supported by wool from Australia.

Based on such facts, Makiguchi, in his seminal work, *A Geography of Human Life,* pointed out the importance of grasping the connection between the world and ourselves through the various goods around us. He described how many of the products he used in his daily life originated in other countries and were generated through the labor of foreigners: clothes made of South American or Australian wool, woven by English labor using the steel and coal of that land; shoes whose soles were made in America, with the rest of the leather coming from India; the lamp in his room burning oil extracted from the Caucasus region of Russia; eyeglasses with lenses produced with skill and precision by German workers. When he examined the various processes by which these products were raised, extracted, gathered, manufactured, transported, and sold before they came to him, he became aware of how his daily life was made possible through the sustained efforts of many people throughout the world. "In this way," he wrote, "I realize that my life extends to and is supported by the entire world, the world is my home, and all nations are the field of my daily life."[7]

In demonstrating the interconnection among the world's people through such examples, he called on readers to appreciate these connections, seeking to lead them toward a life in which people work hand in hand as global citizens to build peace.

REES: The examples given by President Makiguchi are extremely easy to understand, and their contents are something we can relate to. Even though times have changed, the fact that our daily lives are supported by such a connectedness with the world has not changed today.

The Aboriginal poet Oodgeroo Noonuccal, whom I mentioned earlier (see Conversation Three), starts an anthology called *My People* with a poem that imagines an end to racism and a bonding of all people into respect for a common humanity. The poem is called "All One Race." A few lines give the spirit of the poet's vision:

Black tribe, yellow tribe, red, white or brown,
From where the sun jumps up to where it goes down,
Herrs and pukka-sahibs, demoiselles and squaws,
All one family, so why make wars? . . .

I'm for all humankind, not colour gibes;
I'm international, and never mind tribes. . . '

I'm international, never mind place;
I'm for humanity, all one race.[8]

IKEDA: This soulful cry for human harmony by Aboriginal people who have coexisted with nature and lived with pride resounds deeply in our hearts. From conflict in various regions to poverty and the destruction of the environment, our world today faces a proliferation of global challenges. We live in an age when no nation can resolve these issues on its own.

Among these issues, one area in particular that Japan and Australia have been tackling in collaboration is the abolition of nuclear weapons. In 2002, the two countries joined forces with the Netherlands to form the Friends of the CTBT, a group of nations striving to promote ratification of the Comprehensive Nuclear-Test-Ban Treaty. This led to the establishment of the International Commission on Nuclear Non-proliferation and Disarmament in 2008, which published a report to support the international community's efforts toward creating a world without nuclear weapons.

How do you evaluate these developments? What are the key issues in realizing a world free of nuclear arms?

## THE BALANCE OF TERROR

REES: "Eliminating Nuclear Threats: A Practical Agenda for Global Policy Makers" from the 2009 report of the ICNND shows the valuable short-term and longer-term ways—including strengthening the International Atomic Energy Agency's powers and resources—to make progress with nuclear disarmament. I would remind the leaders of nuclear weapons states that possession of such weapons represents the age-old, macho man's idea that he can dominate others because he has the biggest and the most powerful weapons, the "mine is bigger than yours" notion. Such an assumption and the consequent behavior represent acts of cowardice.

The allies of the nuclear weapons states need to emphasize that their security does not and cannot come from having the protection of a nuclear umbrella provided by any so-called great power. These allies need to emphasize the ideals of a common humanity. They need to convince the nuclear nations that weapons capable of destroying the planet must never be used and therefore must be destroyed. I can never fathom why the possession of overwhelming force could be considered a way of winning an argument, let alone be a means of "defense."

IKEDA: The most pressing need is for a change in thinking of the leaders not only of the nuclear weapons states but their allies. I am in complete agreement with your observation.

Although more than twenty years have passed since the Cold War's end, the tragic fact is that the accursed logic of nuclear deterrence persists in a world that clings to the balance of terror, with each side menacing the other. Even worse, it has led to the proliferation of nuclear weapons and a futile arms race.

The only way to achieve genuine peace and security is for both sides to make concessions to eliminate the threat they pose to each other while building relationships to reinforce mutual trust. I long for the day when nuclear weapons states and their allies abandon their policy of nuclear deterrence to create ever-broadening spheres of physical and psychological security that encompass the entire world.

Regarding this point, I recall something Sir Joseph Rotblat of

the Pugwash Conferences on Science and World Affairs shared
with me in our dialogue:

> In the distant past, the security of family was the major
> concern of human beings. Next, people became con-
> cerned with securing the safety of their country. Today, we
> must consciously begin to think in terms of the security of
> all of humankind.[9]

Sir Joseph then cited, as a departure point to initiate a change
in awareness, the principle "If you want peace, prepare for peace."
He stressed his belief that within this mindset lies the conviction
that "there is a way to protect humanity, our most precious common resource."[10]

REES: I met with Sir Joseph about ten years ago (February 2000)
in Okinawa, Japan. It was on the occasion of an international
conference organized by the Toda Institute for Global Peace and
Policy Research, which you founded. I already knew of his inspiring leadership of the Pugwash movement. I felt honored to have
the chance to meet with him in person in Okinawa.

The Okinawa conference left an indelible imprint on account
of his contributions. The great scientist-humanist's observations
at the conference ranged from an insistence that scientists be
concerned with the ethical consequences of their work to proposals for nuclear disarmament, from the idea that atomic research
should contribute to peace to a request that, all around the world,
people should be aware of the catastrophic effects if nuclear weapons were used.

The Toda Institute conference in Okinawa left me with diverse
memories. I was saddened to be face to face with the horrific
details of the loss of life of Japanese citizens and US soldiers in

the battles that marked the end of World War II in the Pacific. I was saddened and frustrated to think that Okinawa must still be the home to a large US military base.

When I visited the Soka Gakkai's Okinawa Training Center in Onna-son village during my visit, I was very impressed to learn that it used to be a US nuclear missile base, and the SGI converted the missile launching pad left on the site into a peace monument. I understand that this idea was proposed by you. If so, thank you so much!

IKEDA: Thank you. I feel as though it was only yesterday that we welcomed you and Sir Joseph, two of our most admired peace champions, to the Okinawa Training Center, engaging in friendly discussions with both of you.

The mid-range ballistic missile Mace B, which could be fitted with a nuclear warhead, was once deployed at that base. An old nuclear missile launching pad with 5-foot-thick, reinforced concrete was left intact, and the Soka Gakkai constructed its facility there. I first visited the site in 1983, six years after the training center's opening, and learned that the missiles' target had been China, and that this site was the only one left standing of the four Mace bases in Okinawa. After visiting the site, I proposed that the bunker, which had been scheduled for demolition, be preserved for all time as a testament that humanity had once engaged in the folly of war and as a pledge never to allow war to happen again. I also suggested to my Okinawan friends that they erect bronze statues symbolizing peace on top of the bunker.

This Okinawa World Peace Monument was completed in 1984, and the missile base that was once a fortress of war was reborn as a citadel of peace, where ordinary citizens share in the vow to build a century without war through the power of the people. Since then, the Okinawa Training Center has welcomed numerous luminaries from the countries that Japan scarred through war, from President Tommy Remengesau Jr. of the Republic of Palau to other distinguished visitors from China and the Philippines. I am happy to report that many left with a favorable impression. For example, President Chen Haosu of the Chinese People's Association for Friendship with Foreign Countries felt that transforming a missile base into a platform for peace was a splendid idea. "I hope many youth will visit this center to learn about the spirit of peace," he concluded.

REES: On my Sydney office wall, I am proud to display a picture of the World Peace Monument, another reminder of the inspired commitment to peace held by the Toda Institute and the SGI.

The biggest obstacles to peace are those values and ways of thinking that almost automatically assume that "might is right," that security only comes from the barrel of a gun. Such militaristic ways of thinking have condemned the globe to centuries of violence. In that sense, too, the transformation from a fortress of war to a fortress of peace has great significance, as shown in such a symbolic way by the World Peace Monument in the land of Okinawa.

In 2010, I composed a poem titled "We Can All Be Grateful" to express our appreciation to those who are working tirelessly for the abolition of nuclear weapons. In that poem, I portrayed two imaginary Japanese girls, one called Hiroshima and the other Nagasaki. They were engaging and clever, and they had been brought up to be full of good humor at all times. Those characteristics defined the humanity that was common to both girls. Time went by, and they both grew up to become leaders and fighters for justice, taking action to promote disarmament. They learned from the tragedies brought to the cities of Hiroshima and Nagasaki, from where their names derived.

IKEDA: It sounds like a truly creative expression on the importance of peace. Surely, it imparts hope and courage to young people striving to rid the world of nuclear weapons in Hiroshima, Nagasaki, Okinawa, across Japan, and throughout the world. More than ten years ago, I contributed to *From the Ashes: A Spiritual Response to the Attack on America,* a collection of essays published in the United States one month after the September 11, 2001, terror attacks. I made the following appeal:

> I feel that a "hard power" approach, one that relies on military might, will not lead to a long-term, fundamental resolution.
>
> I believe that dialogue holds the key to any lasting solution. Now, more than ever, we must reach out in a further effort to understand each other and engage in genuine dialogue. Words spoken from the heart have the power to change a person's life. They can even melt the icy walls of mistrust that separate peoples and nations. We must expand our efforts to promote dialogue between and among civilizations.
>
> I am utterly convinced that we were not born into this world to hate and destroy each other. We must restore and renew our faith in humanity and in each other.[11]

Now is surely the time to dispel the dark clouds of cynicism and mistrust, and advance collectively toward a future of peace and hope.

As an initiative to prompt a decisive change in direction, I proposed that Hiroshima and Nagasaki host the Review Conference of the Parties to the Treaty on the Non-Proliferation of Nuclear Weapons in 2015, the seventieth anniversary of the atomic bombing of those two cities.[12] By bringing together national leaders and representatives of global civil society, the conference would have the character of a nuclear abolition summit marking the effective end of the nuclear era. I presented this initiative in my annual peace proposal in January 2011.[13]

Rees: I strongly support your proposal. Using Hiroshima and Nagasaki as the hosts would be far more than symbolic. It would surely leave an indelible impression on all delegates, an impression that humanity's future depends on a commitment to nonviolence and to disarmament of all kinds.

I clearly recall that after my first visit to the Hiroshima Peace Memorial Museum, I took the famous bullet train back to Tokyo. On that journey, I wondered how to create something in Sydney that would do justice to the experiences of people whose lives had been so drastically changed by the dropping of the Hiroshima and Nagasaki atomic bombs. It was on that journey that I wrote the criteria for the award of Australia's only international prize for peace—the Sydney Peace Prize. One of the criteria for that award refers to a "commitment to the language and practice of nonviolence."[14]

In the passage of your 2011 peace proposal where you proposed the summit for the abolition of nuclear weapons, you stated, "If government leaders together witnessed the realities of the atomic bombings, this would most certainly solidify their resolve to free the world of nuclear weapons."[15] I felt it was an important humanitarian appeal that could be voiced by a Japanese who knows the tragedy of atomic bombings.

Ikeda: Thank you very much. I mentioned earlier how Shirase's expedition to Antarctica was supported by the friendship extended by the Australian people. Antarctica was the first totally demilitarized continent, which obviously includes being nuclear-weapon-free, a status that the international community has unanimously ratified. The Antarctic Treaty that mandates demilitarization came into force in 1961.

Since then, nuclear-weapon-free zones have been established in Central and South America, the South Pacific, and Southeast Asia. In 2009, moreover, the Central Asian Nuclear-Weapon-Free Zone Treaty and the African Nuclear-Weapon-Free Zone Treaty came into force. Nuclear-weapon-free zones now cover most of the land area of the Southern Hemisphere and are expanding to parts of the Northern Hemisphere.

A conference to explore ways to establish a weapons of mass destruction-free zone in the Middle East, which will include the issue of nuclear weapons, is being planned for 2012. The actualization of such a zone will undoubtedly be fraught with difficulty, yet it remains imperative to find a way—not just in the Middle East but also in northeast and southern Asia, where nuclear-weapons-free zones have made little inroad—through tenacious diplomatic effort and dialogue.[16]

Not only is the challenge of eliminating weapons of mass destruction on a global scale a monumental one, so, too, is the task of convincing those who cling to the decades-old belief in nuclear deterrence to redress their belief. The process will certainly be marred by a great many ordeals and obstructions. For this very reason, people of principle have persevered in this effort, and it is why I hope young people—those who must shoulder responsibility for the generations to come—will summon the courage to follow in our footsteps.

Shirase once expressed the passion and determination with which he tackled the Antarctic expedition:

> I want to slog through frontiers never explored before. I detest strolling casually along smooth, level roads where others have cut away the weeds with hoe and sickle.[17]

The challenge is worthwhile precisely because the path is rugged. The joy one feels when prevailing over a challenge and achieving one's goal is that much greater. I will always hope for and expect young people to rise up in high spirits, drawing forth courage with a sublime sense of purpose to enrich and expand the community united in advancing peace for humankind's future.

CONVERSATION EIGHT

# Creating the Conditions for Peace

IKEDA: In Australia, there are nineteen cultural and natural World Heritage Sites registered by the United Nations Educational, Scientific and Cultural Organization, including the Sydney Opera House, a magnificent citadel of art. Many of these heritage sites—such as Uluru-Kata Tjuta National Park, which we discussed earlier (see Conversation Three), and Kakadu National Park—are prized globally for how they combine breathtaking natural splendor and the rich legacy of ancient Aboriginal culture. Cultural sites not only represent invaluable treasures of humankind; for many, they are sacred grounds and spiritual sanctuaries.

Speaking of cultural heritage, in July 2011, the International Court of Justice delivered a landmark judgment concerning the dispute between the governments of Thailand and Cambodia as to sovereignty over the temple compound Preah Vihear, located along the border of the two countries. The ICJ issued a provisional ruling calling for a demilitarized zone around the area, where armed clashes had occurred from time to time, and ordering the immediate withdrawal of military personnel by both nations and the prohibition of all armed activity.

This case shows just how difficult it is to resolve conflict when two parties are in dispute over cultural sites. There are similar cases in various parts of the world, where disputes over and destruction of cultural and religious heritage sites are heightening regional tension and escalating conflict.

Such issues were a focus of the International Conference on Protecting Sacred Spaces and Peoples of Cloths: Academic Basis, Policy Promises, which was organized by the Toda Institute for Global Peace and Policy Research and held in Bangkok, Thailand, in May 2011. Dr. Surin Pitsuwan, secretary-general of the Association of Southeast Asian Nations, and the other scholars and experts who spoke were in agreement that it was not enough merely to avert situations whereby cultural and religious heritage sites are susceptible to attack. They agree we should strive instead to establish a framework of cooperation among neighboring countries to protect the sites, thus enhancing regional confidence.

I think it is vital that initiatives toward peace be rooted in the hearts of the people who live in regions mired in conflict, that they address real-world conditions.

REES: I completely agree with you on that.

In considering the issues of justice and peace, it almost goes without saying that the seminal work of Dr. Johan Galtung, another of your dialogue partners, has influenced my work. His emphasis on structural violence takes us to the sources of social injustice. It reminds anyone struggling to promote a just peace that an end to direct violence is only a small part of the answer. Unless peacemakers address the deep-seated structural causes of injustice—such as those perpetuated by class and caste, by discrimination on the grounds of gender, ethnicity, sexual orientation, or religious affiliation—a just peace cannot be achieved. A peace settlement that ignores structural violence cannot last.

IKEDA: As you point out, structural issues cannot be ignored when seeking to resolve disputes and create a more stable peace. The same holds true with culture: In many cases, the cultural heritage of a region passed on from generation to generation has become integral to the faith tradition and ethnic identity of a group or people in that region, often symbolizing the essence of their community. If others should bear any hostility toward this heritage, and its symbols are damaged or destroyed, the ensuing hatred cannot be readily resolved.

With this in mind, in a dialogue I conducted with German educator and philosopher Josef Derbolav more than twenty years ago, I called for the cooperation of all the world's nations in safeguarding the planet's cultural heritage. I said this in the belief that this cooperation could transcend ethnic and national divides, thereby building a sense of communality and helping to reduce the danger of war.1 Furthermore, open exchange among different cultures tends to become a major source of new inspiration and creation. Given this, the Toda Institute has launched a core research program based on the theme "Engaging the Other"; the international conference in Bangkok was part of this program.

In our dialogue, Dr. Galtung referred to an observation by Benedict de Spinoza that deeply impressed Galtung during his youth: Lack of understanding produces evil, whereas understanding brings good.[2] Spinoza believed that peace is a "virtue that springs from force of character."[3] There can be little doubt that peace will always remain an unattainable dream without the people's proactive will. Moreover, even if a dispute is resolved, unless relationships among the parties rise above merely passive tolerance, rapprochement in its true sense will not be possible; the pathway to peaceful coexistence will surely be barred forever.

REES: The historical record shows that if the terms of a peace agreement have concentrated only on ending hostilities and withdrawing troops, and have not addressed the means of securing social justice, the peace settlement will not hold. The Treaty of Versailles, which ended World War I, is perhaps the best example: Yes, the guns had stopped firing, the carnage had ended, a sort of peace had arrived. But this treaty marked an idea about peace that ignored social, political, and economic issues.

In other words, Versailles marked the victors' version of justice, including massive reparation payments to teach Germany a lesson. In Germans' eyes, it felt like punishment, not justice, and within twenty years, it led to the outbreak of fascism and the beginning of World War II.

IKEDA: It is a heavy lesson of history. As you say, unless there is an effort to realize social justice in conjunction with the effort to seek peace, the cinders of hatred and suspicion will continue to smolder, only to erupt some day in fresh conflict. Throughout history, cultural and religious differences that were at best marginal in everyday life have been fanned for political ends, stoking the fires of animosity that led to numerous disputes and war. This has taken an incalculable toll in irreplaceable lives.

The literary giant Victor Hugo wrote a biting, satirical poem on the history of human strife caused by losing sight of our shared humanity and being blinded by superficial differences:

> For centuries past this war-madness
>    Had laid hold of each combative race . . .

> Each man's hand is raised 'gainst his neighbour,
>    While he strives all his wrath to excite,
> And trades on our natural weakness
> To inveigle us into the fight . . .

> "How dare they from our men to differ,
>    Or venture to wear a white coat!"

"I slay fellow-creatures, and go on
My life's path. What glory like mine?
Their crime is most black and most heinous, —
    They live on the right of the Rhine."[4]

As Hugo incisively observes, history is replete with cases in which war and genocide have been justified and legitimized over the flimsiest grounds, be it that other people prefer white coats, or that they happen to inhabit the wrong side of the Rhine. As members of humanity living in the twenty-first century, we need to learn from the bitter lessons of the past and establish a culture of peace that will firmly take root in every corner of our planet.

## UBUNTU SPIRIT

REES: In that connection, what stands out in my memory is the explanation of the concept of *ubuntu* provided by Archbishop Desmond Tutu, who acted as chairperson of South Africa's Truth and Reconciliation Commission. To young people who will have responsibility for the next generation, I would like to introduce some of his words:

My humanity is caught up, is inextricably bound up, in [other people's].

A person is a person through other people.

I am human because I belong.

A person with *ubuntu* is open and available to others, affirming of others, does not feel threatened that others are able and good; for he or she has a proper self assurance that comes from knowing that he or she belongs in a greater whole and is diminished when others are humiliated or diminished, when others are tortured or oppressed, or treated as if they were less than they are.[5]

*Ubuntu*, a Nguni word, refers to people's interdependence, their common humanity, their oneness with one another and with planet Earth. An understanding of the quality of *ubuntu* is crucial to repair relationships among enemies. It is a quality that refutes an emphasis on individual ego. It means, "I am because you are." Archbishop Tutu's observations about the quality of *ubuntu* are always worth reading and pondering.

IKEDA: They are all worthy insights with which to govern our actions. Coursing through the Buddhist teachings in which the SGI members believe is a view of life that resonates with the *ubuntu* spirit. Shakyamuni's precepts include the following:

Let none deceive another, [nor] despise any person whatsoever in any place. Let him not wish any harm to another out of anger or ill-will.

Just as a mother would protect her only child at the risk of her own life, even so, let him cultivate a boundless heart towards all beings.[6]

When Shakyamuni lived, ancient India was constantly marred by uncertainty and conflict. People resorted to violence out of hatred. Beset by doubt and fear, it is said they wielded weapons even in their own homes. Shakyamuni grieved to see such things, describing such people as "struggling, like fish, writhing in shallow water."[7] He showed the way for people to live together in peace and happiness, teaching them to cherish one another rather than being dominated by hatred and violence.

"'Just as I am so are they, just as they are so am I.' [We] should neither kill nor cause others to kill."[8] There are two important perspectives in this passage. First, Shakyamuni does not attempt to prescribe an individual's behavior through a legal code or other external systems governing human conduct. Instead, he begins with a self-reflective examination based on the vantage achieved when a person embraces the suffering of another as his or her own. As Shakyamuni states, "Just as they are so am I."

Second, it is not enough, in Shakyamuni's view, to merely vow that we ourselves will not kill; we must persist in encouraging others to likewise abstain from killing. I believe it is this inter-action between self-examination and taking action to encourage others—in other words, to constantly reflect upon yourself as you engage in dialogue with others, compelled by your belief in their innate goodness—that will sever the chains of hatred and violence, endowing us with the strength to till the earth from which peaceful coexistence may be cultivated.

REES: That is very thought provoking. When we talk about how to solve conflict and civil war, it is difficult to find fundamental solutions without reexamining the actual way of life of each individual human being.

As I explained before (see Conversation Two), I had been engaged in social work activities before I tackled peace research in earnest. It's easy to see that there's no great distinction between the two fields, though peace practitioners who have not investigated community development or social casework might be surprised by such common ground.

Elise Boulding, whom I would describe as a peace theorist-practitioner, expresses this common ground: "The peacemaker way of life isn't just a state of bliss, but a way of living in the world that deals with all the conflicts and the differences that are part of daily life."[9] That sounds like a social worker's creed.

The Australian peace theorist John Burton also understood my assumptions about the links between the personal and the political, the state, the community, and the family. He insisted:

> Relations between States are essentially no different from the relationships between groups and persons. Conflict and violence are no less a problem at these levels and have the same fundamental sources.[10]

IKEDA: The point you make about how the personal, the political, the state, the community, and the family relate in the task of building peace is crucial. It corroborates what I see as a principle governing people and society: These links and associations, when manipulated by ignoble political interests, can be dangerous, directing people toward conflict and violence. On the other hand, they can facilitate a transformation in individual awareness and create a ripple effect to right social wrongs.

You referred to Tutu's observations. Another champion in the struggle to abolish apartheid, former South African President Nelson Mandela, had these profound insights to share:

> Even at the height of oppression, when racial interaction led to prison and death, we never gave up on our aim to build a society grounded on friendship and common humanity. . . .
>
> Many in the international community, observing from a distance how our society defied the prophets of doom and their predictions of endless conflicts, have spoken of a miracle. Yet those who have been closely involved in the transition will know that it has been the product of human decision.[11]

It was "human decision" that sired the hope to overpower circumstances so onerous that those on the outside saw the transformation as a miraculous feat.

While visiting such communist countries as China and the Soviet Union during the Cold War, I insisted on interaction over division and coexistence over confrontation, and pushed for exchanges in art and culture, as well as education. I did so out of the conviction that all human beings, regardless of nationality, are alike in their yearning for peace, that the way to ease East-West tensions could surely be found.

There is a saying in the East, "Falling drops will wear a stone / Constant dropping wears away the stone." I see no other way forward than to build one sincere, open dialogue upon another, with firm belief in the inherent goodness of human beings.

You worked tirelessly to establish the Centre for Peace and Conflict Studies at the University of Sydney and served as its director for many years before you became involved in the Sydney Peace Foundation. I understand that the Centre has engaged in extensive research into disputes around the world from a broad array of approaches, from policies needed to achieve a just society to the ideals underlying human rights and nonviolence movements, including Gandhi's philosophy and activities. What led to the Centre's establishment?

## A University's Lifeblood

REES: More than twenty years ago, in 1988, a group of social work students at the University of Sydney drew up a petition that said they wanted to study peace, yet there was no opportunity to do so. Even in a great university, peace was not part of any curriculum. The students protested and were aided by a social work lecturer, my colleague Mary Lane. With Mary's clever assistance, the students widened their group to include other interested staff members.

I was professor of social work and social policy at that time and became the mediator/negotiator with the vice chancellor and other university authorities. The first official response was that peace was insufficiently academic to be included in any curriculum. A second response—related to the first—was that "peace studies" did not sound like a university subject.

When I introduced the idea that peace was always linked to conflict, and that conflict had always been studied at universities, the idea of "peace and conflict studies" emerged. This was seen as acceptable. The students' dream began to take shape.

IKEDA: I am impressed. Young people given the opportunity to learn at a university with faculty members such as yourself and Dr. Lane, who put their students before anything else, are fortunate.

Another superb educator, whom we discussed previously (see Conversation Seven), was Sir Edgeworth David, who once told his students:

> To study together these changes, past and present, in the face of the earth, has been our purpose, and in this study we have walked and talked together as comrades. May the friendships and comradeships of this our University life be with us to our life's end.[12]

Students and teachers advancing with humility on the path of scholarship as kindred spirits—this ethos has been part of your university's proud tradition that continues to this day.

I have underscored the importance of such an ethos whenever I speak with the Soka University faculty, stressing that Soka University exists for our students' sake. Our raison d'être lies in their growth and the fulfillment of their purpose in life. I ask that each faculty member take the utmost care of the students, devoting their entire being to the students' tutelage. This student-first education reflects the spirit of the founding presidents[13] of the Soka Gakkai and must serve as the timeless essence of the Soka University.

I am impressed by the spontaneity of the University of Sydney students who launched the initiative. It would be encouraging and instructive for this dialogue's young readers if you would share with us how such an ethos took root at your university.

REES: I shall do so with pleasure. Social work students, who were crucial to the initiative, were encouraged to be proactive on social, political, and economic issues. Encouraging them to take initiative and teaching them the skills of social action was a significant part of their education. The University of Sydney also had a history of students in philosophy and political economy taking action to criticize a conservative curriculum and to promote their more radical interests. In part, such student initiatives followed from the long years of protest against the Vietnam War.

The students' initiative in petitioning for an opportunity to study peace displayed the significance of grassroots—from the bottom up—responsibilities to campaign for social justice. The students' ideas for a Centre for Peace and Conflict Studies have resulted in a tradition of student-centered learning, in teaching that responds to the cultural and social backgrounds and interests of all students. Such student-centered learning also refers to the "promise of biography" concept that we discussed earlier (see Conversation Six).

IKEDA: No matter who the subject of the "promise of biography" may be, human beings are blessed with a wealth of creativity. This is the concept's basis, isn't it?

How do we enable this creativity to come alive and blossom? The enthusiasm and initiative of students, together with instructors who respond earnestly to their students, serve as vital inspiration enabling individual potential to flower. This can be described as a university's lifeblood.

Some years ago (in 1994), the University of Bologna in Italy, which is among the oldest universities in the Western world, invited me to speak. I learned that when the University of Bologna was first established, students were considered their teachers' equals. The original purpose of a university lies in an ethos that encourages freedom and equality in the pursuit of scholarship.

In founding Soka University of Japan, I was aware of the need for an entirely new academic system, one with fundamental questions of our humanity as its starting point. I insisted that the ultimate duty and mission of this university was to address the challenges brought on by this new system.

That is why I set forth the following principles upon its founding:

> Be the highest seat of learning for humanistic education.
> Be the cradle of a new culture.
> Be a fortress for the peace of humankind.[14]

The third founding principle affirms Soka University's role and responsibility as an institution committed to overcoming humanity's bloody history of war and violence.

We will never really know how many people have fallen victim to conflict and war over the millennia. History has shown that whenever war appears imminent, many universities have been transformed into bastions of military research. This is precisely why Soka University must stand with common citizens for all time and fulfill its mission as a citadel safeguarding the people's peace and happiness to the very end.

In 1976, the university established the Peace Research Institute, and in 1987, it began offering a course titled "Crisis and Peace in the Modern Age," later to be renamed "Peace and Human Rights," as part of its general curriculum. We also entered into an agreement with the Peace Studies Department of the University of Bradford in the United Kingdom, which allows Soka University students to pursue peace studies abroad. And we have invited peace scholars from Japan and throughout the world to hold special courses and lectures at our university.

REES: "Be a fortress for the peace of humankind" is a lofty principle. I regard the study of peace with justice as perhaps the most important task in any educational institution.

Spiritually, artistically, and politically, students can investigate inspiring subject matter associated with peace: philosophy and history, poetry and physics, politics and international relations. Such study crosses all discipline boundaries, is relevant to all countries and cultures, and holds great promise for a future humanity. The study of peace and the associated advocacy of peace with justice have great relevance for daily life and for the future of the planet.

Students in the Centre know that in terms of responsibilities to promote the ideals of peace with justice, a lot depends on what they do rather than what they write or say. This confronts students and staff with the question of whether, in vernacular language, they "walk the walk" as well as "talk the talk." The experience of taking action, even in a modest campaign for justice, can have a lasting effect on students' awareness, confidence, and skills.

IKEDA: A sturdy foundation to lead a life of conviction is built through our actions and experiences in the real world. It is especially vital for young people today to expand their knowledge of those individuals engaged in the task of achieving peace with justice and to draw lessons from their lives.

Costa Rica was the first nation in the world to constitutionally mandate the abolition of its armed forces. When I met for the second time with the country's former president, Óscar Arias Sánchez, in December 1995, he shared the following with me:

> My ideal is to abolish all military arms throughout the world. People often tell me that it's nothing but a dream, but we of the Arias Foundation for Peace and Human Progress made it come true in Panama. In the future, I would like to eliminate armaments in Africa and Asia.

The former president has been an equally firm believer in peace with justice, which you helped define and have pursued for many years. In a book he wrote that he was kind enough to present to me, he explains:

> We believe that justice and peace can only thrive together, never apart. A nation that mistreats its own citizens is more likely to mistreat its neighbours.[15]

He also refers to the "structure of state evil" that functions externally to invade other countries and internally to subjugate its own people. Makiguchi and Toda resolutely opposed the militarist regime during the war precisely because they believed that such an iniquitous structure should not be tolerated in Japan.

We must do everything in our power to create a united movement for peace to ensure that all people in any country will never be trampled by the tragedy of war in this century. With this firm resolve, I want to close this chapter with a poem, "The Sowers," by Costa Rican poet Jorge Debravo, whose work former president Arias and I discussed:

> They live to sow.
> Seeds of compassion are in their hearts,
> seeds of hope, and embraces for all people.

Because they understand the bitterness of the earth
they can understand the need to plant new fruit,
so that nobody will walk the streets
bearing loaves of suffering.[16]

CONVERSATION NINE

# Poetry to Reawaken

IKEDA: "[Poetry] is the faculty which contains within itself the seeds at once of its own and of social renovation."[1] So wrote the British poet Percy Bysshe Shelley, the foremost proponent of Romantic literature.

In September 1990, the Tokyo Fuji Art Museum hosted an exhibition titled "The Bodleian Library and Its Treasures" with the cooperation of the University of Oxford, where Shelley once studied. I remember thinking of the poet's turbulent life as I looked at his gold watch, manuscripts, and other artifacts on display.

The 220th anniversary of Shelley's birth was in 2012. The era in which he lived was marked by constant turmoil and upheaval for the European nations. He was born shortly after the American War of Independence and the French Revolution, and his brief life encapsulated the rise and fall of Napoleon Bonaparte. Living through such times, Shelley burned with a passion that can be described as the special entitlement of youth. He aimed for the creation of a more ideal society but insisted that these social reforms must be achieved without recourse to violent means.

In this, he was inspired in part by his travels in conflict-torn Ireland, of which he wrote:

> I do not wish to see things changed now, because it cannot be done without violence, and we may assure ourselves that none of us are fit for any change however good, if we condescend to employ force in a cause which we think right.[2]

Shelley's words epitomize a belief in nonviolence that is said to have influenced Gandhi.

REES: Shelley famously said, "Poets are the unacknowledged legislators of the world."[3] He meant that the values a society should strive for are elucidated by poets.

I have always believed that poets have been some of the strongest advocates of peace with justice. In this respect, poetry has not only the power to influence people with an artistic dimension but has political influence, too.

I frequently use poetry in university lectures and other talks to illustrate issues concerning social policies, human rights, peace, and social justice. I have two main reasons for doing so. First, I feel that the opportunity to be exposed to an art form such as poetry should be offered to as many students as possible and should not be confined to students who might be studying American or Australian literature. I believe that boundaries between subject areas (which become disciplines) are often artificial creations. I am therefore committed to the idea of crossing disciplinary boundaries. Poetry is a beautiful means of doing so.

Second, I want to draw attention to the fact that in almost all countries and cultures, poets write poetry about the circumstances surrounding conflicts. They also use their poetry to promote dialogue in the name of justice and as a means of resolving conflicts.

IKEDA: Be it in the classroom or when confronting manifold social issues, employing poetry to enlighten individuals and inspire people from within is a meaningful endeavor.

In our dialogue, Dr. Harding shared the following on poetry's importance:

> The arts should be at the heart of an education that helps us to become more human. Poetry, especially, gives us some creative ways to think about the story of our lives. This is because poets are constantly trying to reach into the depths of our reality. . . . Poetry can remind us that we have the capacity to create—the capacity of telling and understanding our stories.[4]

Poetry is indeed a fount of immense creativity, offering profound insights into our world's realities and drawing us closer to humanity's true nature. It is from a similar belief that I introduce passages from the world's great poems from all ages whenever I speak with young people on how best to live.

In his essay "The Tug-o'-War in Education," Toynbee argued that it is not enough to provide young people with an education nor to cultivate their abilities. These, he believed, are only "enabling conditions"[5] to draw forth potential. Toynbee envisaged "new humanities" as a curriculum to encourage not only honest improvement in how we lead our lives but also to encourage better relations with our fellow human beings. He asked, "Are not these 'new humanities' likely to minister far more effectively than science and technology ever can to Man's present need to save himself from himself?"[6]

The use of poetry to reawaken the human conscience and reexamine the meaning and purpose of our lives is crucial in achieving an inner transformation of human beings. This is something you have been putting into practice in your work.

## Passion

Rees: I have introduced poetry into the postgraduate peace and human rights educational curricula at several universities, including the University of Sydney, the University of California at Berkeley, the University of Texas at Austin, and the University of Aberdeen in Scotland. My experience has been that students' enthusiasm for poetry overcomes any initial resistance from university authorities who may be inclined to say that poetry is insufficiently academic to be used as a way of commenting on social and foreign policies. I dispute such a claim.

For example, when I called a postgraduate course at the University of Sydney "Passion, Peace and Poetry," a curriculum committee of the relevant faculty objected to the word *passion*. The mood was that such a word should not be officially mentioned in the context of university teaching. However, I would not back down an inch. I insisted that passion is important, and that without passion for learning a subject and without my passion for the students' interests, I could teach very little. As a result, the "Passion, Peace and Poetry" course went ahead as I had insisted and became popular with students wanting to enroll—even with those who said they knew nothing about poetry and thought they did not like "it," whatever "it" was in their previous experience.

Ikeda: I identify strongly with your conviction that one cannot teach anything properly without a passion for learning and a passion for students. This is the same point that Toynbee was making when he spoke of the "compelling power" motivating a human being at a fundamental level; this is education's lifeline.

"Passion" is one of the founding principles adopted by the Soka schools. It was more than forty years ago (April 1968) that the Soka Junior and Senior High Schools in Tokyo, which began as boys' schools, welcomed their first students. The entrance ceremony took place on a magnificently clear, sunny day, and the white school buildings were dazzling beneath the piercing blue skies. The first to enter were 321 high school and 217 junior high school students who had come from all over Japan to study at a school that no one had ever attended before, an institution utterly lacking in history or tradition.

The first thing I did on the day of the entrance ceremony was to join the new students at the unveiling of a stone monument on which were inscribed the words "Wisdom, Glory, Passion." The sight of those gallant students proudly singing the school song that they had just learned remains etched on my mind to this day.

Each year, the Soka schools hold special events to commemorate the Day of Glory on July 17, the Day of Passion on October 10, and the Day of Wisdom on November 18. In 1999, to celebrate the Day of Passion, the students and I welcomed the Italian soccer star Roberto Baggio, who was born the same year that the Soka schools were established and who, on many occasions, faced injuries so serious that they threatened to end his professional career. However, he rose up time after time, driven by his passion for the sport to prevail over every injury.

In my address, I described examples of his struggle and called out to the Soka schools students with the following words in the hope that they, too, would lead victorious lives:

A life without passion is empty. Those who lack the passion to accomplish something, living their days by sheer force of habit, are not really alive. Their hearts are dead. Passion is the proof that we are alive. I, too, have lived my life up to this day burning with passion for my beliefs. I have blazed a trail of victory in the face of countless opponents.[7]

REES: Those words express key principles in life. Truly fortunate are the students who in their youth can store in their hearts the words and visions that contribute to their sense of what is valuable in life, to their sense of soul.

As an educator, I, too, have continued heart-to-heart exchanges with students when teaching at various universities. For example, particularly memorable were postgraduates at the University of California at Berkeley who were enrolled in a class on the history and application of theories of power. These were very bright students who challenged the examination system. I accepted that challenge and abolished exams in that class. The next step was to identify how best to evaluate the students' knowledge, understanding, and skills. We consulted one another. I refused to play the role of a professor who needs to retain control.

Working together, the students in that class chose to write a musical satire as a way to depict the relevance—in California in the mid-1980s—of theories of power in personal relationships and in public life. Each had his or her responsibility, and the performance of a musical satire became the test of the students' knowledge and skills. Twenty-five years later, I am still in close contact with several students from that class.

IKEDA: That is an instructive story. I believe what is important when examining social issues is how deeply we can empathize with the pain and suffering experienced by vulnerable members of society. As such, since staging a performance of the kind you describe requires a person to place him- or herself in another person's situation, it can play an important role in cultivating our imagination, the quality of empathy for others that is demanded of education today.

In fact, I understand that an increasingly important technique in human rights education is the use of role-playing, for example, in simulations and skits—participants vicariously experiencing the abuse suffered by people whose human rights have been infringed—followed by frank discussion to deepen understanding for the victims.

Regarding our capacity for creative empathy, Shelley left us this insightful passage:

> A man, to be greatly good, must imagine intensely and comprehensively; he must put himself in the place of another and of many others; the pains and pleasure of his species must become his own.[8]

Examining this issue from another perspective, the French philosopher Simone Weil stated:

> Compassion is able, without hindrance, to cross frontiers, extend itself over all countries in misfortune, over all countries without exception; for all peoples are subjected to the wretchedness of our human condition. Whereas pride in national glory is by its nature exclusive, non-transferable, compassion is by its nature universal.[9]

An empathetic openness to the sufferings of our fellow human beings is essential to the kind of dialogue that can bring people together, enabling us to transcend the divides and barriers separating cultures, peoples, religions, and ideologies.

Moreover, this spirit encourages people to share in others' misery and embrace it as their own, compelling them to work with those in distress to overcome their plight. Drawing on the language used by Galtung, it not only serves to constrain acts of "direct violence," such as war and killing, but also serves as a driving force to ameliorate "structural violence," such as the poverty, starvation, and discrimination marring society. The role of education in the twenty-first century—particularly at universities—should be to build the foundation on which empathy may be nurtured, a role that must surely rank among education's most cardinal purposes.

REES: I have always encouraged genuine *spontaneity of interest* in others' welfare, others' needs, others' misery or happiness. But a question remains, how do you do this?

When I speak with different groups about their main concerns for their families and communities, I usually ask at some point, "Do you want to make your life more interesting?" Almost everyone answers "yes" to that question.

I then ask, "How do you think you could make life more interesting and, at the same time, promote your mental and physical health?" In answer to that question, my respondents begin to address the choices of working only for our own interests (the inward-looking approach) or making a commitment to others' well-being (the outward-looking approach). People of all ages are challenged by the idea that personal fulfillment that includes an outward-looking approach to life can contribute to physical and mental health.

I'll put that point another way: I'll refer to John Donne's poem that begins "No man is an island, entire of itself; every man is a piece of the continent, a part of the main."[10] In those memorable lines, the poet was implying "I am because I am able to contribute to others' well-being in addition to my own." I suspect that even the most selfish of young people would be impressed by those ideas.

## Compassionate Empathy

IKEDA: Through caring deeply about the plight of the distressed and taking action for their happiness, our existence shines with meaning, and our humanity deepens. The health of society as a whole will improve as more and more people dedicate themselves to this process. This ideal is resonant with the Buddhist way of living.

In a letter to one of his followers, Nichiren wrote:

> What does Bodhisattva Never Disparaging's profound respect for people signify? The purpose of the appearance in this world of Shakyamuni Buddha, the lord of teachings, lies in his behavior as a human being.[11]

Bodhisattva Never Disparaging, who is described in the Lotus Sutra, engaged in the practice of bowing to each person he met out of genuine respect, based on the teaching that the Buddha nature exists equally in all people.

This illustrates that the purpose for which Shakyamuni appeared in this world was to teach how we should live. Shakyamuni underscored the importance of waging an impassioned struggle against indifference and the lack of compassion that constantly seek to invade our hearts while taking action for people beset by worry and woes amid the world's harsh realities. He taught that there is no other way to lead a genuinely meaningful, worthwhile life.

Shelley also brought to the fore the necessity of battling against mercilessness and apathy:

> It will not be kept alive by each citizen sitting quietly by his own fireside, and saying that things are going on well, because the rain does not beat on him, because he has

books and leisure to read them, because he has money and
is at liberty to accumulate luxuries to himself. Generous
feeling dictates no such sayings.[12]

How are we to conduct ourselves in order to surmount the
inclination toward indifference and lack of compassion pervading
modern society?

According to Nichiren's teachings on the Lotus Sutra, "'Joy'
means that oneself and others together experience joy."[13] The SGI
members have sought to remain true to this message, striving to
triumph over the innate proclivity to service one's own interests
without regard for others' needs. In heeding the cries of the tormented, we have continued to pray for their happiness as well as
our own and worked to better all our lives.

Despite enduring unjustified maltreatment and persecution
over the years, we have never wavered in our belief that the
supreme state of life, or Buddha nature, expounded in Buddhism
exists within all human beings. We have stayed engaged in serious,
sincere dialogue. And we have continued to care for and treasure
everyone we know, endeavoring to extend this ethos throughout
society.

REES: Yes, I am reminded, after being engaged in social work
over many years, that it's not always easy to find the energy to
keep going. But it's always rewarding to engage with people. Their
appreciation that another human being is taking them seriously is
usually a reward in itself.

I feel that I am fortunate to have good health and to have lived
in affluent, developed countries. In this respect, I have an obligation to make an effort to assist others who, when their lives
began, were not given such a good start in life as that which I
enjoyed, from my parents and from my country's educational

and health-care systems and from an economy that generated job opportunities.

In my encounters with many people through my social work career, my happiest experiences occurred with African Americans in the War on Poverty programs in the States. We laughed a lot about the absurdities and injustices of racism; they teased me about being white. We valued one another's friendship; we exchanged numerous stories about our families and our hopes for the future. They were funny, energetic, and very loyal. I remember and value those qualities and my time with them.

My social work background and experience taught me that if you want to know how people live, how they feel, how they speak, how happy or sad they are, how fit or sick they are, there is no substitute for face-to-face encounters. It is the case that people living in deprived areas are usually voiceless, unable to express their grievances, let alone obtain appropriate services. In this respect, my usual question at the end of interviews—"Is there anything else you want to say; is there anything you wish to ask?"—gives an opportunity for the voiceless to have a voice.

Nobody feels bad about being asked for his or her opinion. This is even more the case for people who have been passed over by society. In fact, those questions are always appreciated. I also discover people's humor even in the most demanding and depressing circumstances. Such human spirit—expressed through humor and hospitality—is so encouraging.

I have enjoyed the generous hospitality of very poor people— such as untouchables in the slums of Mumbai—who welcomed me to their clean but crowded, slumlike homes.

IKEDA: While the Soka Gakkai is an organization of ordinary people, it was the object of considerable uninformed criticism during its pioneering post-war days, often derisively described as a "gathering of the sick and poor." When told of this, however, President Toda would caustically note, "How many unhappy people have those detractors helped, then?" As a friend to and ally of those enduring the greatest hardship, the Soka Gakkai has imparted courage and hope to hundreds of thousands, even millions, of people: This is the hallmark of our history. No one, regardless of who they may be, should ever be discriminated against or deprived of their pride and dignity as a human being.

Oodgeroo Noonuccal made this poignant declaration in "A Song of Hope":

> Look up, my people,
> The dawn is breaking
> The world is waking
> To a bright new day
> When none defame us
> No restriction tame us
> Nor colour shame us
> Nor sneer dismay.[14]

This "bright new day" of hope will never dawn over humankind unless we establish a society in which all are equally accorded their dignity and can lead fully humane lives. As a global, grassroots organization emerging from the great earth of ordinary people, the SGI has engaged in the struggle for the world's voiceless as its overriding mission, a struggle that we have proudly embraced over the years.

While I have met with political leaders and leading thinkers abroad, I have also placed the utmost value on heartfelt exchanges with ordinary people on my travels. During the Cold War some forty years ago, in September 1974, I first visited the Soviet Union. My recollection of a woman my wife, Kaneko, and I came to know at the hotel where we were staying remains vivid to this day. On each floor of the hotel, there was an employee in charge of the room keys, and she was looking after our floor. At first, she was unsmiling, treating us in a fairly businesslike manner. Nonetheless, my wife and I exchanged a few friendly words with her every day through our interpreter as we deposited or collected our keys. Bit by bit, she became friendlier and started to talk to us with a smile.

One day, she asked us in a friendly way: "You visited the Supreme Soviet in the Kremlin today, didn't you? It was broadcast on the television news earlier."

I confirmed that she was correct and told her that after visiting the Kremlin, we placed flowers on the Tomb of the Unknown Soldier. We had seen an elderly couple weeping in front of the tomb, I told her. "It was very tragic. I am firmly opposed to war and will do everything I can to prevent it from ever happening again."

The woman lowered her eyes and said softly, "My husband also died in the war." She then said, "Please create a world without war," as if she was entrusting me with her heartfelt desire.

I vowed to her to do my best for peace. "I hope you'll also work for peace," I urged. "Your voice will help change the world."

This was just one of my many encounters—not only in the Soviet Union but throughout the world—that I cherish to this day. Only through steady, often unseen efforts to engage in sincere, one-to-one dialogue with an open heart and mind is it possible to expand the community of ordinary people united in the pursuit of peace. This is the SGI's spiritual legacy that has been passed down without the slightest deviation since the days of Makiguchi and Toda.

As Shelley called out:

> Rise, like lions after slumber,
> In unvanquishable number,
> Shake your chains to earth like dew,
> Which in sleep had fall'n on you.[15]

The only way to banish the tragedies brought on by war and violence, and end the tyranny and discrimination is to bring people together in "unvanquishable number." For this purpose, the SGI members remain firmly committed to humanistic education, which nurtures in people a boundless capacity for compassionate empathy. We will continue to promote it as widely as we can.

CONVERSATION TEN

# Fighting for What Is Right

IKEDA: Jessie Street, the Australian activist who strove for many years to advance the rights of women and Aboriginal peoples, and improve their status in society, once made this impassioned declaration:

> There are small victories and bigger ones in the struggle against discriminations. But the real goal is recognition of the principle of equality.[1]

People embracing and practicing equality will serve as the foundation for a new society of peace and harmonious coexistence.

At the end of 2011, the United Nations General Assembly adopted the UN Declaration on Human Rights Education and Training, which aims to inspire and enhance human rights awareness among as broad a constituency as possible. It calls for every government, intergovernmental organization, NGO, and international society to provide education and training in the spirit and significance of our basic human rights—from the inherent dignity of human beings to freedom and equality as enshrined in such documents as the Universal Declaration of Human Rights.

The 2011 declaration does not limit human rights education to the mere acquisition of knowledge and technical skills; it defines human rights education as a lifelong process involving a transformation in the way we live and in our behavior toward others, applied in the course of our social activities. The declaration serves as a global guideline clarifying the basic principles and objectives that every nation needs to adopt to nurture a human rights culture.

Dr. Rees, your work to promote human rights education among young people has contributed greatly to the advancement of this human rights culture.

REES: I've always regarded the Universal Declaration of Human Rights as the most significant document of the twentieth century. It sets a standard for the conduct of civilized relationships in any country or culture. Education about the grand vision and small print of this document, about the rights and responsibilities described in each of its thirty clauses, could be a condition for every student who graduates from high school or at least from university.

Such education about human rights is exciting because it challenges people to think about their own identity, to consider the ways they use authority and the manner in which power is exercised in relationships, in the home, on the streets, at work, or in any context.

In other words, the interpretation of and respect for human rights is with us every waking hour. It's not just an expert's responsibility and certainly should not be left to lawyers. It's a challenge for all of us.

IKEDA: The SGI has devoted much effort to promoting human rights education; it is a core activity of ours as an NGO affiliated with the United Nations, an endeavor predicated on Buddhist philosophy, which places great weight on the inner transformation of every individual. The SGI's representative at the United Nations in Geneva, serving as the chair of the NGO Working Group on Human Rights Education and Learning, worked closely with other NGOs to ensure that civil society's views were reflected in the drafting process of the UN Declaration on Human Rights Education and Training.

Establishing laws and regimes to protect human rights is obviously essential. Even more paramount, however, is the need to instill and foster in every person an abiding spirit fully committed to protecting the dignity of life. Without this, human rights will always remain an unattainable ideal.

Gandhi declared: "Non-violence is not like a garment to be put on and off at will. Its seat is in the heart, and it must be an inseparable part of our very being."[2] Only when human rights norms become a personal vow—the sense that unless I hold to these, I can no longer be myself—do they become an inexhaustible energy source for social transformation.

REES: I, too, believe that emphasizing the dignity of every individual human being is the key to understanding the Universal Declaration of Human Rights and provides a clue to the meaning of each of its thirty clauses. If all citizens were accorded dignity by the state and by other individuals, it would hardly be necessary to insist on the rights to freedom of expression, to freedom of movement and residence, to education, to social security, to work and to leisure.

Also, I have a conviction that young people's education about human rights begins in the home. If there is a genuine observance of the dignity of family members, and if family life is conducted in a spirit of love and freedom of expression, of respect for shared responsibilities and for individual differences, these qualities will serve as an excellent basis for human rights education. In this sense, it is profoundly significant that the international community work together to promote the UN Declaration on Human Rights Education and Training.

## THE RIGHT THING TO DO

IKEDA: The family can be described as a child's first school. In this sense, too, the parents' approach to and behavior in everyday life are very important.

I have had the opportunity to speak with many of the world's foremost thinkers who have distinguished themselves in their chosen fields over the years. A large number of these men and women have told me that they are what they are today largely because of the influence of their parents' beliefs and way of life.

Dr. Francisco J. Delich, who served as rector at both the University of Buenos Aires and the National University of Córdoba in Argentina, is one such person. At a time when a military junta had unleashed a storm of human rights abuses in Argentina, Dr. Delich was among those who refused to yield to government pressure and intimidation, persisting in a principled battle of words to expose the plight of his fellow Argentineans to the world.

He was the youngest of eight children born to an impoverished farming family. When I asked about his parents during our meeting in Nagoya, Japan, in April 1994, he shared his precious memories: "My parents always worked very hard. The sweat of their brows taught us the rigors as well as the nobility of hard physical labor. My mother was illiterate, but she had a wisdom all her own." He said, "My mother taught him two things: first, it is wrong to make money without working for it; and second, it is important to show respect for others by never telling lies."[3]

Although many Argentineans opposed the military junta's campaign of human rights abuses, most felt they had no choice but to remain silent. To Delich, however, this was further justification for his decision to speak out and fight back, forging ahead upon the path of utmost resistance despite being forced to endure constant police surveillance. He was supported in his struggle by the underlying spirit of his mother's two lessons—namely, that he must never stray from the true way of life that human beings should lead, regardless of the circumstances in which he might find himself.

"Thinking was forbidden, speaking out was forbidden," he recalled. "How painful this is for human beings! I think that Soka Gakkai members, who have also been oppressed by military authorities in the past, understand what I am talking about."

As he spoke, the crimson light of an August sunset poured into the hotel room where we met. The tone of his voice was calm, but I could sense the depths of his dedication to his cause, as well as the enormous torment that he underwent, and felt my heart flush with emotion.

Later in his life, one of his children asked him, "Father, why did you choose the path of resistance at that time?" His answer was short and to the point: "Because it was the right thing to do."[4]

REES: Listening to your anecdote brought to my mind Harper Lee's *To Kill a Mockingbird*, which I read in my youth. Against the background of the 1930s slump that was triggered by the Great Depression, the novel portrays a lawyer who lives up to his beliefs, and his children. It is a masterpiece set in the southern state of Alabama, where discrimination against black people was very strong.

The main character is the lawyer Atticus Finch, who stood up to defend and prove the innocence of a black man alleged to have raped a white woman. Atticus was criticized even by his own relatives in a town where racial discrimination was routine, and he prepared himself for the fact that he had little chance of winning. Nonetheless, he undertook the defense and expressed to his younger brother his feelings about it: "Do you think I could face my children otherwise?"[5]

Before long, the callous gaze of the entire town toward Atticus spread to his son, Jem, and daughter, Scout, who were ridiculed by their classmates and neighbors. At that time, Atticus sat his daughter on his lap, put his arms around her tightly, and said:

> It's not fair for you and Jem, I know that, but sometimes we have to make the best of things. . . . This case, Tom Robinson's case, is something that goes to the essence of a man's conscience—Scout, I couldn't go to church and worship God if I didn't try to help that man. . . .

> Before I can live with other folks I've got to live with myself. The one thing that doesn't abide by majority rule is a person's conscience.[6]

As you know, this novel was made into a movie, in which the main role was played by Gregory Peck. The novel is an inspired piece of writing.

In a similar vein, a superb biography of a wonderful lawyer, the fearless Clarence Darrow, is titled *Attorney for the Damned*.[7] Darrow defended many poor and powerless people and often did so without asking for a fee. He knew all about human rights well before the signing of the Universal Declaration.

I would very much like people to open their eyes to the fact that the injustice called racial discrimination is still widespread on every continent. To confront injustice, to attain justice, requires courage, knowledge, and skill.

IKEDA: History teaches us that society has made the progress it has today because there have been people who literally risked their lives battling the social iniquities threatening human rights, and that justice in any era can only be achieved through the struggle against injustice. Every word uttered by Atticus Finch resounds with great weight, does it not? As a parent, he did not want to live in such a way that he couldn't face his children. More than anything else, he sought to live without feeling ashamed.

His words are neither grandiloquent nor honeyed. They reflect the flesh-and-blood conviction that wells forth from personal character. Even as he finds himself about to be engulfed by the dark depths of despair, he doggedly stays true to the path he has chosen; he shines with the courage to forge ever onward.

Speaking of trials, as a young man I was once detained for two weeks on false, baseless charges in what has become known as the Osaka incident.[8] After my release, my struggle continued in the courtroom. Even my defense attorney was fatalistic, going so far as to say it would be difficult to overturn the prosecution's allegations, despite my innocence. He told me to expect a guilty verdict.

Nevertheless, I was prepared to fight the charges to the very end. Shortly before Toda passed away (on April 2, 1958), he said to me: "The trial will not be an easy battle. It may trouble you for some time to come. But you will win in the end. For gold is gold; it never loses its luster no matter how it may be muddied. The truth will definitely come out. Just fight with dignity and courage"[9] He spoke these words as he struggled to get up from his sickbed, and I took them to heart over the four years and three months I waged my legal battle. His words resounded like the roar of a lion mustering its last breath, and they gave me limitless courage and conviction.

Of the eighty-four court hearings, I appeared twenty-three times. The trial continued even after my inauguration as third Soka Gakkai president (on May 3, 1960), the post I assumed succeeding my mentor. I was finally acquitted in 1962; the final ruling came on a fine, bright winter day.

Obviously, it was important that the truth of my innocence had finally been validated. For me, however, the greater honor was that by clearing my name, I ensured that the reputation of my mentor and the Soka Gakkai had not been tarnished in the slightest, and that I had repaid my debt of gratitude as Toda's disciple.

REES: A court battle that went on for four years and three months? I admire your stamina and courage, and that of your wife and family and friends.

Although I'm not familiar with the operation of Japanese law, I'm somewhat cautious about the motives of powerful people and powerful institutions. I spent many years in my early career working in courts of law in Britain and Canada. I was not always certain that the individuals who represented "authority" could be relied on to seek justice. Darrow would have advised me that it was all a piece of theater, usually dramatic, always stressful, often sad, but for many citizens triumphant in the end. You were one of those citizens.

It does sound as though you and your wife found the stamina and courage to resist the prosecution and emerge with your name and reputation intact. A crucial period in your life?

IKEDA: Yes, I believe that Kaneko's struggle, supporting me both in public and private, was nothing short of herculean.

Recalling those days, my eldest son once remarked:

> I have no unpleasant memories whatsoever of the Osaka incident and the legal struggle that happened when I was a child. Although the criticism and slander against my father and the Soka Gakkai was incalculable, I never felt

any sign of such strife when I was at home. Looking back on it now, that was all due to my mother.

And that has not been the only occasion: Throughout the years we've been married, Kaneko has been selfless and unwavering in her support. My feelings of gratitude to her know no bounds.

To return to our earlier discussion, both as an educator and a man of action committed to peace and humanitarianism, in what ways have you called on your students to build a society that places utmost importance on the dignity of the human being, to realize "peace with justice"?

## Transformation of the Age

REES: I have always considered that education about human rights begins and depends on a culture of hospitality and tolerance, of support and interest, of dialogue and diversity. Once students recognize and can contribute to such a culture, then the notion of human rights can be easily understood and applied.

Apart from that, whether it is a political, economic, or social question, I have regarded it as important to have an attitude to break boundaries, reject stereotypes, and acquire a new understanding. Meetings with most students generate the energy necessary to prompt key questions about their lives, about themselves. I encourage them to question conventions, to challenge assumptions, to develop a fascination with discovery and with learning. I have devoted myself as an educator to opening a path toward that end.

IKEDA: As you have stressed, the courage to become fully aware of the realities of discrimination, human rights violations, and other issues, and the courage to delve seriously into these issues—this courage becomes the launchpad for the creation of value and can ultimately transform the age.

Makiguchi once stated:

> We must strictly avoid following ideologies of uncertain origin that cannot be substantiated by actual proof—even if they may be the most time-honored tradition—and thereby sacrificing the precious life of the entire community of self and others.[10]

He made this call around the time of the Pearl Harbor attack (in December 1941), when Japan was plunging headlong into the mire of war.

Since ancient times, there has been a pronounced inclination among the Japanese to avoid as much as possible questioning whether something is good or bad. Such sayings as "Don't try to stand against the tide" and "Look for a big tree when you want shelter" epitomize a spiritual climate of prioritizing self-protection and self-interest rather than weighing what is good or bad, right or wrong. One can argue that this ethical vacillation endemic to Japanese society was what opened the door to the rampant rise of militarism, resulting in the unilateral, barbarous invasion by Japan of its neighbors abroad and the stifling of freedom of speech and suppression of human rights at home.

The philosopher Edward Wadie Saïd offered the following analysis:

> In no country more than modern Japan has the interplay between the imperatives of the collective and the problem of intellectual alignment been so tragically problematic and vexed.[11]

Under such unforgiving circumstances, Makiguchi strove to right Japan's wrongs by intrepidly raising his voice in objection.

REES: In this modern day and age, people strongly seek the courage displayed by Makiguchi. The tendency to be swayed by the current of the times, which in turn is influenced by the authorities, or to choose self-preservation out of fear of power is still seen not only in Japan but also in the politics and public life of many countries.

On this point, a poet whom I value is the American poet Marianne Moore, who passed away about forty years ago. In several poems, she described the courage required to speak out. When I'm confronted with a need to challenge powerful people and institutions, I can usually gain inspiration by returning to lines from Marianne Moore's poems.

For example, in "Blessed Is the Man," she appears to identify that crucial quality of courage to be expressed by all citizens and especially by poets:

> blessed is the author
> who favors what the supercilious do not favor—
> who will not comply. Blessed, the unaccommodating man.[12]

The way of life advocated by Moore through her poems echoes the assertions of the British playwright Harold Pinter, who was the subject of our earlier discussion (see Conversation One).

Further, on the topic of opposition to war, the poem "Men" by the American poet William Stafford sticks in my memory. It's a powerful satire about the absurdity of war and the failure of powerful leaders to learn the lesson that violence only begets violence, that war only produces grief and requires massive human and environmental costs. In this poem, he speaks of women and children having to remember the stupidity of war; that powerful men learn nothing and in consequence can only think of preparing for the next destructive conflict.

IKEDA: I recall that Stafford was a conscientious objector during

World War II. Dr. David Krieger, the president of the Nuclear Age Peace Foundation, with whom I shared many discussions some time ago, was a young conscientious objector during the Vietnam War. He told me that was when he began to commit to being a peace activist.

I understand that, at the time, Krieger was criticized as disloyal to his country and a coward for challenging the military and refusing to fight. His wife's parents, who belonged to the generation that had fought in World War II, did not look kindly upon him. However, he stood firm in his convictions to the end.

In our dialogue, Krieger looked back on those days and had these words for the youth of today:

> In questions of life and death, no one should entrust the decision to another person or to one's government. Nor should one be swayed by public opinion. It is up to individuals to decide for themselves on the basis of conscience.
>
> I hope to teach young people the lesson I learned so that they can avoid the struggle I experienced. If enough young people learn the lesson, we can do away with wars.[13]

REES: I think this is a truly important message to the young generation who are going to shoulder the future. David Krieger is a good friend of mine, so I value and understand your example, the story of David's conscientious objection.

In my youth, I deepened my ideas about overcoming war and violence by reading *The Life of Mahatma Gandhi* by Louis Fischer and *War and Peace,* the great novel by Leo Tolstoy. In Fischer's book, I was particularly impressed by passages describing Gandhi's insistence on the peaceful and painful refusal to obey evil governments, hence the subsequent philosophy of nonviolence and civil disobedience. The reason I mention Tolstoy's *War and*

*Peace* is because it remains one of the most powerful indictments of the stupidity of violence and war.

## POWER OF PERSUASION

IKEDA: Be it the poems of Moore and Stafford you cited earlier or *War and Peace*, literary works whose every word and thought are underscored by their authors' principles and deeds are alive with an indefinable element that never fails to stir the depths of our souls. I also agree with your point that storytelling is vital in communicating a message. The political theorist Hannah Arendt concurs with you as well in her powerful declaration "No philosophy, no analysis, no aphorism, be it ever so profound, can compare in intensity and richness of meaning with a narrated story."[14]

In the same way, the Buddhist scriptures that are foundational to our beliefs in the SGI feature numerous parables that answer the question of how we ought to live, as well as provide ways to perceive the truth about society and phenomena. The Lotus Sutra contains seven such parables.[15]

For example, in the parable of the three carts and the burning house, a father resorts to "expedient means" to save his children who, engrossed in play, are oblivious to the fire that has engulfed their house. He skillfully coaxes them out of the flames.[16]

The parable of the wealthy man and his poor son, meanwhile, tells the following story: The son of a wealthy man runs away from home as a young man. Over a period of several decades, he travels through many regions, forced to endure a life of great poverty. Eventually, he comes by chance to his father's mansion. The son does not recognize that the master of the mansion is his father, but having recognized his son, the father comes up with a plan. He decides to employ his son, starting as a cleaner. The son works with sincerity and gradually gains self-confidence. After more than twenty years, he reaches the point where he is entrusted with administering his father's estate.

The father is relieved to see how his son has turned out. As the father senses his own death approaching, he invites the king and his ministers to the house. He tells them, "This is my son, who ran away from my house a long time ago. I am going to entrust every-thing to him."[17] His son then realizes the truth for the first time and comes to understand the constant love and consideration his father has had for him.[18]

These two parables illustrate that the purpose of Buddhism is to awaken people to the boundless potential they possess within their lives, and that human life is irreplaceably precious, endowed with the "cluster of unsurpassed jewels."[19] I believe what defines these two stories is how they both depict a gradual transformation in another's heart with total respect for the other's autonomy and inner-motivation.

There may be a way of life to which we wish people would aspire or a great truth we feel they ought to pursue, but these can-not be unilaterally imposed by external force or through change so rapid that it leaves people unconvinced. The message of these parables is that we must at all times uphold deep respect for each individual's right to come to those realizations for themselves, and that we should extend support and encouragement to them as they learn to act with their own heartfelt conviction.

REES: That is an extremely important approach. In various situa-tions in my life, I have attached great importance to the "realiza-tion" you have emphasized, for example, encountering inhumane or outrageous events, or events so beautiful, I have felt the need to take and make poetic pictures of them.

I have also benefitted from the impact and inspiration gained from reading and pondering excellent poetry and literature. For example, Moore wrote another poem in which she imagines how a caged bird can sing:

> Though he is captive,
> his mighty singing
> says, satisfaction is a lowly
> thing, how pure a thing is joy.
> This is mortality,
> this is eternity.[20]

From this poem, I feel strongly the message that hope can be conjured even under the most trying circumstances. But I know that I'm a fortunate citizen who has enjoyed rewarding employment. I'm not poor, sick, and unemployed. Conjuring hope under difficult circumstances is a much greater challenge.

There is someone I respect who promoted this understanding and who for many years was an active and significant citizen in Australia. I'm referring to the late Dr. Stella Cornelius, the founder of the Conflict Resolution Network, which was established in 1986 with the support of the United Nations Association of Australia. She lived and breathed the principles of nonviolence. Until her dying day—she passed away at the end of 2010—she taught the principles of conflict resolution, mostly by example.

Dr. Cornelius was efficient and generous, and never spared herself in working on others' behalf. The work of Dr. Cornelius and of Faith Bandler, who led the campaign to ensure that Aboriginal Australians became citizens, was acknowledged by President Nelson Mandela when he visited Sydney. In the corridors of The University of Sydney's Centre for Peace and Conflict Studies, there is a happy photograph of Nelson Mandela embracing these two great women.

Dr. Cornelius had a habit of encouraging people to say *and* rather than *but*, as if the optimism that follows *and* is more likely to solve conflicts than the pessimism often introduced by the word *but*.

Ikeda: As you say, one often hears people say things along the lines of "I can understand the importance of world peace, but it will be difficult to achieve." Implied in qualifiers such as "but" in statements like this is a feeling of resignation and acceptance of the status quo. On the other hand, if one were to say, "World peace is necessary, *and* to this end, let us create a solidarity of ordinary people that transcends national borders," within the word "and" lies the courage and conviction to advance, even a little, to change things for the better while remaining mindful of the difficulties.

As for the youth who must bear the twenty-first century on their shoulders, my hope is that they will persist upon the latter path—to embrace a challenging yet supremely meaningful life. I encourage them to engage others in dialogue, live out their lives among the people, and persevere in the struggle for peace to the very end. There is no other way.

With this wish, I wrote the following in a poem titled "Dance of Youth, Song of Youth":

> Knowing no limitation,
> within your breast
> lives the vivid heartbeat
> of your struggle.
>
> Within that sturdy beat
> lies the power
> to shatter all constraints.
> You have the belief and courage
> that will enable you, calmly, to transform
> even the stifling embrace of the crowd—

even the suffocating, frosty embrace of cunning—
into flames
that will blaze a trail.[21]

My mentor often used to ask: "What does it mean to be young if you cannot make a difference? What does it mean to live if you do not add a chapter to history? Achieve something! Leave something worthy behind!"

It is my abiding wish that young people will come together, and that this united community will vigorously expand to build a world where the dignity of all people can shine, where all may live in peace and happiness. Young people have a crucial role to play.

CONVERSATION ELEVEN

# Dignity for All

IKEDA: "It is absolutely wrong to sacrifice the individual for the prosperity of society. As society prospers, so too must the happiness of the individual increase."[1] These are my mentor's unforgettable words.

The world economy is facing a serious crisis ostensibly triggered by the collapse of Lehman Brothers in 2008. The situation remained grim in Europe and the United States for a long time, while Japan was saddled with a massive deficit, even as it was mired in a deep, persistent recession.

In my annual peace proposal in January 2010, I took up unemployment, brought on by the economic crisis, as a major cause of instability in society, and urged that remedial steps be taken as quickly as possible, especially regarding jobs for young people:

> Young people, in particular, can be deeply affected if they are unable to find work or abruptly lose their jobs soon after joining the workforce. In addition to financial difficulty, they can be scarred with feelings of lack of worth

and of insecurity concerning the future in such a way that
can even undermine the will to live. At the same time,
human dignity is gravely threatened when individuals are
employed under inhumane or degrading conditions, or if
lack of job security makes it impossible to plan realisti-
cally for the future.[2]

Unemployment is one of the issues with which you have grappled over many years, as you work for social justice.

REES: Persistent unemployment is one of the major social injustices of today, and it pushes people into a condition that signifi-
cantly threatens dignity—almost the same as making them social
outcasts. In considering this problem, what come to my mind are
stories and pictures about the misery caused by long-term unemployment in the Great Depression that began in 1929. The pictures are depressing. The stories are accounts of powerlessness
and match the pictures.

In *The Road to Wigan Pier*, his account of unemployment in
Lancashire coal mining districts, the British writer George Orwell
gave graphic depictions of the poverty caused by unemployment.
He described overcrowded living conditions, malnutrition, personal misery, ill health, families' experiences of cold and hunger,
and their desperate search for fuel and food.

In those days, the economist John Maynard Keynes showed
how unemployment could be addressed by appropriate government intervention. His theories were applied in the economic
policies of several countries; recently, such Keynesian-type inter-
ventions have been referred to as economic stimulus packages. In
this respect, the fatalism that nothing could be done about unemployment had been overcome. However, there is no change in the
fact that the effects of unemployment remain serious, for individuals and for the chances of building or rebuilding a civil society.

IKEDA: Robert Zoellick, president of the World Bank, suggested in an address in Sydney in August 2011 that the global economy has entered a "new danger zone"[3] with the Eurozone being shaken by the debt crisis in Greece; this and other crises threaten to undermine the very foundations of the global economy. Around the world, the contraction of available credit and decline of the real economy are adversely impacting employment.

The jobless rate among young people is serious. More than 45 percent of young Spaniards and 38 percent of young Greeks are unable to find work, and one in five young people are said to be without jobs in the United Kingdom, where riots occurred in London and other cities in August 2011.[4] It is also a mounting concern in Japan.

REES: In a book I edited along with Gordon Rodley and Frank Stilwell, *Beyond the Market: Alternatives to Economic Rationalism*, I once stressed as follows:

> The right to the dignity of work should be a basic human right for all citizens. A growing number of people are losing this right. These people are being denied the profound human sense of self-worth that comes from work; either in the sense of earning one's keep, having the satisfaction of achieving something, or making a contribution to society.[5]

In other words, I stressed that unemployment should not be regarded as a mere economic problem but as an issue that threatens human dignity at the core and deprives people of purpose and opportunities for self-fulfillment.

IKEDA: This point should never be overlooked. Among the employment policies implemented by various countries to date, which has attracted your attention most?

Rees: More than anything, I should say that the New Deal programs of President Franklin D. Roosevelt had a dramatic effect on citizens who had previously experienced the depression and long periods of unemployment, eroding their self-esteem. The crafting of a range of accessible and dramatically beautiful national parks in the United States is a lasting tribute to the success of this New Deal experiment.

Ikeda: The dam construction scheme of the Tennessee Valley Authority is one of the best-known New Deal projects. At the same time, the Civilian Conservation Corps hired many jobless young people in the effort to develop and maintain national and state parks and forests. As a result, it is said that three million young people were engaged in CCC activities over a period lasting some ten years, and that more than two billion trees were planted in that time, leading to remarkable progress in many areas for the National Park System.

In launching the CCC, President Roosevelt declared,

> It is my belief that what is being accomplished will conserve our natural resources, create future national wealth and prove of moral and spiritual value not only to those of you who are taking part, but to the rest of the country as well.[6]

This presidential initiative was not simply an economic measure undertaken by the government; what I believe to be more significant is the fact that, as you pointed out, it enabled people to regain their self-esteem. The sense of purpose and pride in knowing that your work is of service to society and the future is an irreplaceable source of encouragement.

Rees: Evidence in Australia suggests reasonably high motivation among most young people to obtain meaningful employment.

However, the opportunities to obtain rewarding employment are limited. The number of young people seeking such opportunities is not matched by available jobs.

Also, in Australia, homelessness is a serious problem. Young people's unemployment is associated with homelessness and with unsupported living conditions, as in cases of broken families. In such cases, young people become homeless or are pushed into more serious poverty. Opportunities for education and training become important in order to encourage such vulnerable young people to participate in society and contribute to it.

IKEDA: In recent years, as social inequalities in Japan have intensified, a growing polarity has developed between those who earn large incomes and lead stable lives and those who are forced to live in economic distress as a result of deteriorating employment conditions.

On this point, I recall a conversation I had with the economist John Kenneth Galbraith, who lived through the tragedy of the Great Depression of the 1930s. He insisted that people who have lost their jobs due to factors beyond their control and are experiencing misfortune as a result should never be stigmatized by society for their loss. I wholeheartedly agree with him.

Society must extend a safety net for those who have lost their jobs, providing them with a measure of economic stability. And we need to establish a society of hope and security, in which the jobless will consistently have the opportunity to rebuild their lives.

Dr. Galbraith made it clear to me that a key task for the twenty-first century will be establishing an era in which people can honestly say, "I enjoy living in this world." Creating job security and workplace environments that do not abuse human dignity are integral to such a world.

Regarding one program to help those without work, I remember Dr. Galbraith said: "when people are now unemployed—as I once read in a Japanese paper—you have them painting the

schoolhouse door. But in fact, they should be painting a painting."
The point he was making was that people can draw fulfillment and
joy from work with a measure of creativity rather than work as a
mere means of sustenance.

We know of many people who have grappled with serious difficulties yet lived without losing their dignity as human beings.
Society must strive to support such individuals, so that they can
continue to live with more hope and greater purpose in life.

## Efficiency

Rees: One major theme that has characterized the work of the
University of Sydney's Centre for Peace and Conflict Studies concerns the principle that no one should be financially penalized for
being sick. This may seem like an obscure comment in a discussion about peace. In fact, it refers to the ideal that the availability
of universal health insurance is a peace with justice issue. We have
campaigned to protect universal health insurance in Australia.
This also applies to the issue of unemployment.

In November 1998, the University of Sydney co-organized an
international conference on the theme "Socio-Economic Security: Globalization, Employment, and Quality of Life" with the
Toda Institute for Global Peace and Policy Research. The themes
that the creation of employment opportunities is a major peace-
with-justice goal and that persistent unemployment is an injustice
continue to characterize the Centre's identity and values. Those
themes and questions about the interdependence of human
rights and quality of life gained great emphasis from that 1998
conference.

I have great respect for Dr. Galbraith, whom you mentioned
earlier. His famous saying about a free market leading to private
opulence and public squalor[7] placed great emphasis on the civi-
lizing influence of a well-supported public sector in any society.

Another advocate of the Galbraith school of thought was my friend and mentor at the University of Sydney, the late Professor Ted Wheelwright. Ted identified the influence of large corporations in generating wealth for their own benefit but not caring about the environment, let alone human rights. The worldwide protests about corporate greed and the occupation of financial centers in the world's large cities in October 2011[8] suggest that the ideas of professors Galbraith and Wheelwright are being converted into action. Wheelwright argued that societies should be measured more on what they contribute to people's personal development and happiness and less on how efficiently they provide goods and services.

IKEDA: The English word *economics* is *keizai* in Japanese, a contraction of the original word *keisei-saimin*, which means "bringing order to society and easing the suffering of the people." The philosophical principles underlying this word resonate with Wheelwright's insights.

In my youth, I received instruction from Toda on an extensive range of disciplines, from politics and economics to law, world history, astronomy, and life philosophy. In the beginning, he tutored me at his home on Sunday mornings; in time, we held sessions every morning at a company he managed, where I also worked, just before we opened for business. The first of his early-morning lectures was on economics. At the core of every lecture, regardless of the subject, was his fervent belief that war and social iniquity, which plunge people into the depths of grief and misery, were utterly unacceptable.

I recall one session on economics, in which he elaborated on the nature of inflation:

> The term "inflation" is customarily defined as a state in which the price of goods is continuously increasing.

When thought of in that way, stabilizing prices becomes the primary objective of policy.

However, what happens if this state is viewed from the perspective of ordinary people? If inflation is defined in terms of the hardship caused to the general public, the primary policy objective is not price stabilization but how to ameliorate the pain and suffering of people. This should be the perspective that governs economic policy.

This was why Toda was unrelenting in his criticism of politicians indifferent to ordinary people confronting difficulties.

Every endeavor, be it politics, economics or culture, exists to serve the happiness of human beings. Since the daily lives of ordinary people, every single individual, are directly affected by politics in particular, politicians should always see matters from a broader perspective and never become swayed by narrow self-interest or the profit of a specific group, nor become blinded by the pursuit of short-term gain.[9]

His words remain with me to this day. A mathematician and educator, he also managed a publishing business and other enterprises. However, given the post-war chaos, there was a time when his business ventures teetered on the verge of collapse. With the outbreak of the Korean conflict, the ailing Japanese economy managed to stage a recovery thanks to demand for war-related procurement. Many companies posted enormous profits as a result, but he adamantly refused to listen to those who urged him to exploit the cresting boom in war-related demand, rejecting that path as perverse and unethical.

REES: That really illustrates his unshakeable conviction; it makes a profound impression on me. I have always harbored a strong doubt about the word *efficiency*, which is often used in economics. Claims about efficiency are easy to make because they tend to ignore social considerations.

When reverence for free market economic policies influenced government policies from the 1970s onward, the emphasis on efficiency followed. It was so easy for politicians, leaders of industry, and the heads of universities, hospitals and welfare organizations to recite the mantra of efficiency. If you only emphasize efficiency, you don't have to think very much. In reaction to this reverence for efficiency, I made several radio broadcasts saying I was in favor of inefficiency if this meant caring for people, not profit, if it meant having regard for people's health and well-being rather than their alleged productivity.

Hearing the voices of those who are usually not consulted is perhaps the most important strategy to achieve a sense of social justice in any society or organization. But the advocates of economic efficiency have tended to assume that hospitals could be run without consulting patients, universities could exist irrespective of students, libraries could operate without people who borrow books, and even factories could be managed without much reference to the views of shop-floor workers.

IKEDA: It appears that the pursuit of efficiency only grows stronger as the economy deteriorates. It also seems that this becomes a frequent cause of major rifts or imbalances in human society. When society loses sight of higher purposes and aimlessly seeks economic profit and efficiency, deep contradictions and manifold vulnerabilities are bound to emerge: wealth disparity, divisions among peoples, a general loss of resilience to rebound from every adversity. This is the stark trajectory that we see in the crises we confront today.

The Indian economist Amartya Sen, working on the reformulation of economics as an ethical philosophy, has long warned of a growing gap between economic principles and the ethical frameworks that support people and society. In his work *On Ethics and Economics,* Dr. Sen advances his argument with a quote from Aristotle: "The life of money-making is one undertaken under compulsion, and wealth is evidently not the good we are seeking; for it is merely useful and for the sake of something else."[10] In this way, Dr. Sen is calling for a revival in economics from the perspective of how human beings should lead their lives, and how we can achieve good in society.

In April 2001, Dr. Sen delivered a lecture on economics at a symposium organized by the Ikeda Center for Peace, Learning, and Dialogue, which I founded in 1993 in Cambridge, Massachusetts. During the series of conferences and lectures on the theme of "Economics for Human Well-Being: Advancing a People's Agenda," Dr. Sen posited that the degree of progress and development made in the richness of human lives is contingent upon the degree of freedom that people enjoy. He further argued that the key in achieving development lies with the intrinsic human drive to be free. I believe there are points of commonality between Dr. Sen's argument and Buddhist philosophy, which assigns great weight on the inner transformation of human beings.

## POVERTY AND HUMAN RIGHTS

REES: Amartya Sen's notion that people's freedom is a crucial measure of development reminds us of the intermingling of social with economic systems. His study of welfare economics mirrored and influenced the United Nations' introduction of the Human Development Index, which—to assess a country's progress—uses measures in areas closely related to human dignity such as literacy levels and the number of children in school. I respect Amartya Sen for the same reasons that I'm grateful to Dr. Galbraith and Professor Wheelwright. There is an essential humanist quality in Amartya Sen's work.

I have always felt that we also need to identify why economic systems have come to dominate social values and social systems. That imbalance and the means of regaining the right balance between economic systems and social values are fit subjects for study.

In my travels in the world over many years, I have seen cases of people being sacrificed for economic gain. There are numerous examples. When I stayed in India in 2010, I was saddened to see women on a building site slaving in temperatures higher than 100 degrees Fahrenheit, carrying large numbers of bricks on their heads. Clearly, the Western world's view of health and safety measures in the workplace does not apply where the treatment of labor depends on a free market. In developing countries, for example, powerless poor people can be exploited and their exploiters never held accountable.

Respect for universal human rights needs to become the priority means of fighting poverty. This support for human rights needs to replace the usual preoccupation with economic growth. If that change occurred, the idea that people are commodities who can be sacrificed for economic gain would be eroded, just as earlier forms of slavery were eventually abolished.

I have previously mentioned the international conference co-organized by the Toda Peace Institute and the University of Sydney. A future Toda Institute conference could address the issue of "Poverty and Human Rights." Massive poverty remains such an appalling violence against vulnerable people. The persistence of poverty and the associated abuse of human rights are large obstacles to global peace with justice.

IKEDA: These are key points when discussing peace and human rights issues. In essays I have contributed to newspapers and through my annual peace proposals, I have also issued strongly worded warnings on the widening divide between the rich and poor, as well as on the pervading disdain for human rights. I have long held that this "stark disparity in the value of human life and dignity, virtually predetermined by where one is born, is an unconscionable injustice in global society that must be corrected."[11]

With regard to the Millennium Development Goals called for by the United Nations, an international initiative to solve poverty and other issues, I have stressed that the "effort to achieve the MDGs must be focused on not only meeting targets but also restoring the well-being of the individual who is suffering."[12] I thus heartily endorse your proposal to position respect for universal human rights at the core of redressing poverty and find your approach vital and viable. I believe this problem can only be resolved when we undergo a fundamental transformation in our values.

As you know, Dr. Sen witnessed a great famine that swept through his homeland of Bengal during his childhood, which he has said motivated him to study economics and engage in research to prevent the recurrence of the tragedies caused by poverty and famine.

As you pointed out, lurking under the poverty issue is how human egoism and greed lead some people to become all too eager to exploit others for personal profit. Buddhism describes base impulses—the functions of greed, anger, and foolishness, which are intrinsic to human life—as subverting our core virtues and plunging us into unhappiness. There can be no fundamental solution to all these manifest issues unless we confront and overcome this deeper, underlying problem.

Toda's fervent wish, as I have mentioned previously (see Conversation One), was to eliminate the word *misery* from the human lexicon. The mission of the Toda Institute for Global Peace and Policy Research, which draws its inspiration from Toda's vision and values, is to banish the specter of poverty, famine, and other threats that torment humanity by bringing together the world's wisdom and insights for every human being to shine with dignity.

By working closely with you, Dr. Rees, the Toda Institute aims to further broaden the reach of the network of peace with justice that you have established. And as we focus on the plight of the poor, the victims of human rights abuses, and the grim realities faced by the most vulnerable members of society, the Toda Institute is committed to the development of solutions to better our world.

# Altruism Over Egoism

IKEDA: Toda often used to say, "The Earth is a living entity." We have now entered an age in which the world's population exceeds seven billion. When I was inaugurated as third president of the Soka Gakkai in 1960, the world's population was three billion—it has more than doubled in half a century.

In 2011, Babatunde Osotimehin, executive director of the United Nations Population Fund, stated, "A world of seven billion is both a challenge and an opportunity." He has stressed that "new ways of thinking and unprecedented global cooperation" are required for "reducing inequities and finding ways to ensure the well-being of people alive today—as well as the generations that follow."[1] I concur, and many people are in agreement on this. If we remain set in our conventional ways of thinking, we cannot ensure our planet's well-being.

I also recall that Toda, more than fifty years ago, said: "One day the Earth's population will reach six billion, and we'll be faced with a whole new set of problems. The leaders of our world must start seriously thinking about our planet and humankind from now."

REES: Conventional ways of thinking have produced market-based civilizations. These are the kind of societies across Europe and the United States that now experience huge social and economic inequalities and related social problems, such as homelessness and large-scale unemployment.

Conventional ways of thinking have worshipped individualism—the idea of every person for him- or herself. Such a way of thinking ignores the benefits of investment in the public sector and ridicules the goal of striving to share benefits equally. Such shortsighted perspectives are the opposite of those that laid the foundations of civil societies in post-war Europe, Australia and New Zealand, and, I imagine, Japan.

IKEDA: The inequities facing people alive today to which Dr. Oso-timehin referred can be described as various distortions in society, including politics and the economy. Among these distortions, poverty is a particularly pressing concern. In the world today, more than 25 percent of the total population still endure extreme poverty.[2]

It has been reported that the number of people suffering from poverty has been on the decline due to such efforts as the United Nations Millennium Development Goals. Nevertheless, instead of being preoccupied solely with achieving the numerical target of halving poverty rates, we must not forget to direct our attention to the plight of all needy individuals, so they may secure opportunities to brighten their lives and regain their sense of hope.

Dr. Mohammad Yunus, the founder of the Grameen Bank, who I believe is your friend, has devoted himself for many years to eradicating poverty. He has defined extreme poverty as a "disease which has a paralysing effect on mind and body"[3] and which leads to "the absence of all human rights."[4]

REES: I have great respect and affection for Dr. Yunus. He was the inaugural recipient of Australia's only international prize for peace, the Sydney Peace Prize established by the Sydney Peace Foundation. At that time, in 1998, his theories and the practice of microcredit were not well known. He has told me that the Sydney award gave much needed publicity to the Grameen Bank.

Through the Sydney Peace Prize and our close association and dialogue with its diverse recipients, the Sydney Peace Foundation has been promoting awareness of the challenges that require concerted efforts of the international community. For example, we focused on the awful predicament of child soldiers when Ambassador Olara Otunnu[5] won the Sydney Peace Prize in 2005, raised awareness of the urgency of nuclear disarmament when Swedish diplomat Hans Blix[6] received the prize in 2007, and stressed the influence of the media in countries' knowledge of injustices when distinguished Australian journalist and filmmaker John Pilger won the prize in 2009.

By the same token, our dialogue with the distinguished recipients of the foundation's Gold Medal has also produced inspiring occasions and lasting memories and friendships. Those recipients, including former president of South Africa Nelson Mandela and you, Mr. Ikeda, have stressed the ideals of a common humanity, the priceless value of peace with justice, plus the vision and courage required to achieve such goals.

IKEDA: It was a great honor and privilege to receive the Gold Medal from your foundation in April 2009. I was also most grateful for your heartwarming citation at the conferral ceremony.

At that ceremony, I quoted Dr. H. V. Evatt, an Australian jurist and legislator who studied at the University of Sydney and helped draft the Universal Declaration of Human Rights: "We certainly want peace, but we want peace with justice—a peace that shall afford to all persons in all countries positive opportunities to live full and happy lives."[7] His words dovetail with the principles of humanitarianism that surge within the Sydney Peace Foundation.

Which areas of Yunus's work have you focused upon in particular?

REES: Three criteria impress me about Dr. Yunus's work:

1. The initiative in making almost all his loans available to women, who traditionally had no entitlement to open bank accounts let alone receive loans.
2. The use of grassroots, village-based committees to oversee the use of the loans and to support the people who, on the basis of the loans, are trying to generate new businesses, new means of livelihood.
3. The emphasis on the social benefits to be obtained from microcredit rather than the profits to be gained by individuals or organizations.

In this respect, the Grameen Bank seems to work according to that influential value—the dominance of altruism over egoism—that I have referenced in earlier conversations.

## REAL-LIFE ECONOMICS

IKEDA: Each of these points can be described as groundbreaking in that they are consistent with the sublime principle of protecting the poor.

Some time ago, I met Anwarul K. Chowdhury, former Bangladesh ambassador to the United Nations and subsequently UN under-secretary-general. He gave me some woven fabric hand-decorated with fine embroidery by women who had achieved independence utilizing microcredit. Chowdhury said that this beautiful artwork, while in a traditional Bangladesh design, represented the struggle of poor women of the present. From this woven fabric, I strongly felt the pride and confidence of women who have embarked upon a new path.

As you pointed out, the prime achievement of Grameen Bank's activities lies in opening a path of economic independence for women who suffer from poverty. Until now, the banking world has invariably refused to even consider extending credit to many poor people, especially women, who were unable to provide collateral and who could not read or write.

This kind of prejudice remains deeply rooted in society, and Yunus was exposed to considerable criticism. "The poor enjoy serving their masters rather than taking care of themselves," he was told, and that "by extending credit to women, the traditional role of women in the family will be adversely affected. . . ."[8] However, Yunus shattered those prejudicial attitudes. He and his colleagues strove tirelessly to explain the purpose of microcredit to villagers, while doggedly supporting the women borrowers who managed to regain joy in their lives as they acquired confidence and hope.

Yunus stated:

> I firmly believe that each human being is an unexplored treasure. Each person has unlimited potential. . . . [B]y being a producer and contributor to the world's well-being she or he has enormous possibilities.[9]

As they become more invigorated, women can brighten the lives of entire families and infuse entire villages with energy. Yunus has witnessed such transformation time after time and describes efforts to finance women as creating a "cascading effect."[10]

REES: It is a precise expression. I think that the practices and culture of the Grameen Bank have the potential to free women from the shackles of religious and male-dominated customs. The discriminatory views on women asserted by opponents of the microcredit system have similarities with the ideas of those who may not like to see the promotion of the awareness of human rights, which we discussed in the previous conversation.

Such ideas often hold that traditional cultures will be destroyed if universal human rights are achieved. It is merely a myth and, incidentally, is usually promoted by men who are reluctant to give up their discriminatory and violent ways of treating women. In this respect, let me repeat my appreciation of your advocacy of the education of girls as a twenty-first-century priority in your annual proposals.

IKEDA: Jessie Street has astutely pointed out,

> One thing I feel sure of is that any society that does not encourage the development and use of the brains and abilities of all its women as well as its men will become a sterile society.[11]

She is absolutely correct.

Ever since Makiguchi's time, the Soka Gakkai has emphasized educating women and taken steps to advance their education. The key to social reform and progress lies in women's vibrant activities.

Thinking about the deep prejudices toward poor people that Yunus has striven to uproot, I remember that Toda would often admonish us to never judge people by appearances. Economic distress is undoubtedly terrible, but nothing impairs a person's dignity more than being scorned and neglected by society.

When Toda was young, he once paid a visit to distant relatives who were wealthy. Having recently arrived in Tokyo from the far cooler Hokkaido, he was wearing a padded cotton jacket and shabby *hakama* (traditional Japanese trousers) despite the approaching summer. Although the family did not turn him away, they looked him up and down dismissively. They listened to what he had to say, but it was clear that they had no wish to be associated with him and wanted him to leave quickly. He never forgot his sense of chagrin.

I understand his feeling. In my youth, I used to work at a printing company while attending night school. Among my duties was dragging a large cart through the streets to deliver printed materials to publishers in the Ginza and Kanda areas. Between the weight of the materials and the stifling heat, I was often bathed in sweat.

The Soka Gakkai was born among ordinary people and has come to flourish because it is firmly rooted in ordinary people's lives. This is precisely why President Toda declared: "The Soka Gakkai stands on the side of ordinary people; we are a friend of the unfortunate. No matter how others may scorn or scoff at us, we will fight on for the people's sake." It was a struggle that he carried out to the very end.

As a disciple who has wholeheartedly embraced Toda's struggle, I have acted with the same spirit. I remember back in 1974, when I was about to embark on my first visit to China, reflecting on the Soka Gakkai's humble beginnings and saying to the people who came to Haneda Airport to send me off, "I have managed to come this far with you, those of us who were derided as 'the sick and poor,' without having to rely on political influence or financial resources."[12] This was more than forty years ago—two years after diplomatic relations between China and Japan were finally normalized, in 1972.

The Soka Gakkai has always reached out to the most troubled and the most miserable. By encouraging one another and by working together, we have forged lives of hope and courage. As a result, ordinary people have boldly spoken out against the injustices of society and striven to better their communities at the grassroots level. This is our greatest pride.

Rees: Your account has deepened my understanding of where the Soka Gakkai's identity is rooted.

And you have just mentioned the history of poor women in Bangladesh being long excluded from lending services. Similar economic isolation and marginalization exist in developed countries, and their damage is aggravating in scale. It is these people, excluded from banks' lending activities, who are being forced to pay the largest costs of the recent global economic crisis, despite the fact that they are not responsible for causing it.

The absurd respect for the so-called freedom of the market, the greed of Wall Street, and the similar greed of developers and speculators in property markets appear to have produced the worldwide economic crisis. I therefore agree with Mr. Makiguchi's ideal of humanitarian competition, which you introduced earlier (see Conversation Two). His vision to serve others as well as ourselves remains inspirational. It keeps in mind those values and relationships that affect people's quality of life. It is grounded in concern for the practicalities of daily living. It appeals to me because it echoes the principles that have affected my teaching and my advocacy of public policies.

Those principles concern the notion that policy should be about the triumph of altruism over egoism, that support for strangers without counting the costs (the "gift relationship") is a bedrock goal for families, for schools, for society at large. In all those respects, I value Mr. Makiguchi's teachings and am grateful for his legacy.

Ikeda: I'm sure that Makiguchi would be overjoyed to know that someone of your stature has such an appreciation for his ideas. Makiguchi surmised that while military conflicts are temporary, occasional, and deliberate, economic conflicts can be permanent, constant, and often unintentional. He thus sounded this warning:

Mediation by third parties, whether individuals or organizations, is possible only in military conflicts. In economic war, the battles usually continue until winners and losers are irreversibly determined through competition.[13]

In the case of military wars, there is room for mediation to halt the ravages from spreading. But no such brakes exist in the case of economic wars. Makiguchi warned that the tragedy of the latter, which is based on the rationale that the weak are invariably victims of the strong, is destined to unfold without end. In contrast to the obvious cruelty brought about by war, he pointed out that the inhumanity perpetrated by economic rivalry could easily be overlooked precisely because of its daily, mundane nature. This is where so many of the sources of the disease afflicting modern society lie.

REES: That is a very insightful observation. When I reflect on the consequences of economic competition in endless pursuit of wealth, I am reminded of the poem William Wordsworth composed as he witnessed the drastic industrialization caused by the Industrial Revolution in nineteenth-century England.

> That to an idol, falsely called "the Wealth
> Of Nations," sacrifice a People's health,
> Body and mind and soul; a thirst so keen
> Is ever urging on the vast machine
> Of sleepless Labour, 'mid whose dizzy wheels
> The Power least prized is that which thinks and feels.[14]

Wordsworth warns that humanity disappears when greed motivates employers and workers. Such employers and workers, he says, end up worshipping a "false idol."

In today's society, the economy has been extensively affected by the foolish interpretations of freedom assumed by economic speculators, politicians, and financiers. Freedom should mean responsibility as well as personal motivation. It should mean commitment to the well-being of one's neighbors as well as concern with one's individual and family interests.

I would stress the following three mechanisms for ensuring that the current world economic crisis that started in 2008 is cured and not repeated:

1. Domestic and international economic policies should be influenced by the UN Conventions on Economic, Social and Cultural Rights and by the Convention on Civil and Political Rights.
2. Belief in private enterprise must be balanced by investment in public-sector institutions and services. A society needs to be judged by its civility and commitment to social justice not by the number of billionaires and by the extent of economic growth and corresponding economic inequality.
3. Citizens' security is achieved by policies reflecting the two aforementioned points and not by a country's readiness to go to war. Commitment to nuclear disarmament and to a drastic lowering of defense budgets would facilitate the building of a vibrant public sector—better public schools and public hospitals—and could simultaneously have beneficial effects on the environment.


IKEDA: If I have understood you correctly, the economic policies that are needed in the future must therefore be developed from the standpoint of human rights, social justice, and peace based on disarmament. Policies that lack such clear philosophical and doctrinal bases and merely emphasize economic expansion and growth will not lift the heavy burden of those suffering from economic disparity and destitution.

In the past, based on Makiguchi's concept of humanitarian competition, I have urged a transformation to shared or mutual value-creation instead of the "eat or be eaten" ethos of competition. If we speak of economics in this context, what is needed is a constructive economy in which people can provide value for one another, as opposed to an economy in which people scramble over ownership of one another's assets. In other words, we need to make the transition to an economy that enables all human beings to create value.

After Bangladesh gained its independence in 1971, Yunus returned home from the United States, where he had been studying, and began teaching at a university. However, he later confessed:

> I used to get excited teaching my students how economics theories provided answers to economic problems of all types. . . . But when I came out of the classroom I was faced with the real world. Here, good guys were mercilessly beaten and trampled. I saw daily life getting worse, and the poor getting ever poorer.[15]

When Yunus's country was ravaged by famine, and he witnessed numerous people starving to death, he realized the impotence of the economic theories that he had been so proud of teaching. This experience led him to "discover the real-life economics."[16] He went out to a nearby village, canvassing its inhabitants to cull insights into the causes of their distress. It was then that he began nursing the idea to finance women living in poverty.

Later, in order to expand the reach of his microcredit initiative, Yunus travelled to villages rife with armed insurgents. Unfazed, he continued to meet with villagers and held numerous discussions with them. In the end, his perseverance paid off as some young guerrilla fighters laid down their guns and joined his microcredit staff, triggering a new wave of social change. Yunus described his feelings at that time: "[The People's Army] in Tangail had a lot of fighting spirit waiting to be channeled in the right direction, why not give them a chance to do something constructive for society?"[17]

The responsibility of providing young people with opportunities to create new ways and new initiatives rests entirely on those entrusted with leadership.

## SMALL VICTORIES

REES: Based on many years of experience in social work and conflict resolution, I feel that a positive catalyst or a solid sense of reward is essential in prompting people to start a new way of living. I will continue with unwavering commitment to work for people's empowerment, so that they can take control of their lives.

My experience tells me that the transformation from being dependent to enjoying independence goes through stages. The first stage concerns the need to overcome that fatalism that suggests that nothing can be done. A second stage concerns the beginning of trust among those who are working together. A third stage is to generate resources and to teach skills, which could cement this trust and start to make a difference in people's lives. I'm a great believer in a philosophy of small victories, and every stage reached and passed is a small victory.

IKEDA: I agree with all you say. In our dialogue, Peccei shared his thoughts on the limitless potential of human beings:

There exists in each individual a natural endowment of qualities and abilities that have been left dormant but that can be brought out and employed to redress the deteriorating human condition. . . .

The innate, vital resourcefulness and intelligence intrinsically inherent in every human being, from the most talented and fortunate to the most deprived and marginal, constitute the unequalled patrimony of our species.[18]

These thoughts and convictions resonate deeply with the SGI's beliefs. Founded on the principles of Buddhist humanism, our movement of empowerment of the people, by the people, and for the people is now active in 192 countries and territories.

Judith Wright, whom you mentioned is one of your favorite poets (see Conversation Three), once wrote, "You can't get happiness from anywhere outside your own being; it comes from first obeying your own inner truth, and it's only then that you begin to live."[19] The transformation of every human endeavor begins with a transformation within a human life—a truly "human revolution."

Buddhism holds that the noblest state of life exists within all people's lives equally, and that through the practice of faith, we can manifest compassion and wisdom, creating value and substantive changes in our environment and society in ever expanding waves. The global SGI movement's history may be described as proof of this.

In society today, a sense of powerlessness—the feeling that nothing will change, no matter how much effort one makes—is undermining people's hearts in significant ways. When faced with reality and its myriad difficulties, people are robbed of hope and become trapped inside their own small worlds. I cannot help but think that herein lies the root cause of suffering in the modern age. We must fight against such forces of negativity. Now is the time to create a united community of ordinary people of the world, a surging union with which to challenge our weaknesses and overwhelm them in resounding fashion, reaffirming our belief in our ability to prevail over every trial and adversity.

There is a verse from Australian poet Mary Gilmore that rings deeply in my heart:

> Out of the dark
> Still comes the light
> And day is born
> In the deepest night.
> Take courage, then,
> Be not forlorn;
> For though night fall
> Yet comes the morn.[20]

In a world that seems to be inexorably sliding into the depths of chaos and uncertainty, this powerful poem inspires us with courage that transcends space and time.

I hope to continue cooperating with you, Dr. Rees, whom I hold in the highest esteem, so that we may advance together toward the sun of hope majestically dawning over humankind's future horizons. I will make every effort to ensure that peace with justice will take root and flower in every corner of our planet. I am profoundly delighted and honored by this opportunity to take part in this meaningful, illuminating discussion with you and to share it with the world's youth, upon whose shoulders rests our collective fate. Thank you very much indeed.

REES: It has been inspiring for me to have witnessed your promotion of international dialogue over so many years and with so many international figures. I have also been educated and inspired when reading your dialogues with these significant world citizens. Each of them has made invaluable contributions to the service of humanity, and each has obviously enjoyed the opportunity to be so closely engaged with you.

In all these respects, I have also been privileged to have several face-to-face conversations with you. In addition, our exchanges in these conversations have revived my optimism about the future, despite the trends about which we have each spoken.

Thank you so much for your leadership, your poetry, vision, and courage. I hope that the respective organizations that we lead will continue to be close allies, and that what we have discussed will make a difference to many readers in many societies, in many people's lives.

# Selected Works
## Daisaku Ikeda

*America Will Be!: Conversations on Hope, Freedom, and Democracy* with Vincent Harding. Cambridge, Mass.: Dialogue Path Press, 2013.

*Into Full Flower: Making Peace Cultures Happen* with Elise Boulding. Cambridge, Mass.: Dialogue Path Press, 2010.

*Journey of Life: Selected Poems of Daisaku Ikeda.* London: I.B. Tauris & Co. Ltd., 2014.

*A New Humanism: The University Addresses of Daisaku Ikeda.* London: I.B. Tauris & Co. Ltd., 2010.

*Our World To Make: Hinduism, Buddhism, and the Rise of Global Civil Society* with Ved Nanda. Cambridge, Mass.: Dialogue Path Press, 2013.

*A Quest for Global Peace* with Joseph Rotblat. London: I.B. Tauris & Co. Ltd., 2007.

*Reaching Beyond: Improvisations on Jazz, Buddhism, and a Joyful Life* with Herbie Hancock and Wayne Shorter. Santa Monica, Calif.: Middleway Press, 2017.

APPENDIX 2

# Selected Works
Stuart Rees

*Achieving Power: Practice and Policy in Social Welfare.* Crows Nest, Australia: Allen & Unwin, 1991.

*Beyond the Market: Alternatives to Economic Rationalism.* Edited by Stuart Rees, Gordon Rodley, and Frank Stillwell. Melbourne, Australia: Pluto Press Australia, 1993.

*The Human Costs of Managerialism: Advocating the Recovery of Humanity.* Edited by Stuart Rees and Gordon Rodley. Melbourne, Australia: Pluto Press Australia, 1995.

*Passion for Peace: Exercising Power Creatively.* Kensington, Australia: University of New South Wales Press, 2003.

*Tell Me The Truth About War.* Charnwood, Australia: Ginninderra Press, 2004.

*Practicing Non Violence: Gandhi Legacy, The International Priorities.* Sydney: The Sydney Peace Foundation, 2013.

# Notes

## Preface by Daisaku Ikeda

1. This dialogue was originally serialized in Japanese in *Daisanbunmei*, a monthly magazine, June 2011–May 2012.

## Preface by Stuart Rees

1. Published in 2010, *Time for Outrage!* is the English translation of the thirty-two-page *Indignez-vous!* (in French), which sold nearly a million copies in its first ten weeks and was subsequently published in thirty languages.

## Conversation One
## Peace Is Not Only The Absence Of War

1. The Great East Japan Earthquake—this magnitude 9.0 earthquake and subsequent tsunami struck eastern Japan on March 11, 2011. It was the strongest earthquake known to have hit Japan and the fifth most powerful in the world. There were reported to be 15,883 deaths and 2,667 missing throughout twenty-two prefectures.

2. In 1983, Daisaku Ikeda began writing peace proposals and sending them annually to the United Nations. The publication date each year is January 26, the anniversary of the founding of the Soka Gakkai International. These proposals offer perspectives on critical issues facing humanity, suggesting solutions and responses

grounded in Buddhist humanism. They also put forth specific agendas for strengthening the United Nations, including avenues for the involvement of civil society.

3. See Daisaku Ikeda, "Toward Humanitarian Competition: A New Current in History," 2009 peace proposal, in *A Forum for Peace: Daisaku Ikeda's Proposals to the UN*, ed. Olivier Urbain (New York: I.B. Tauris, 2014), pp. 311–342; also at http://www.daisakuikeda.org/assets/files/pp2009.pdf.

4. John Milton, *The Complete Poems of John Milton*, vol. 4, ed. Charles W. Eliot (New York: P. F. Collier & Sons, 1909), p. 405.

5. John Forster, *The Life of Charles Dickens*, vol. 1 (London: J. M. Dent & Sons Ltd., 1948), p. 16.

6. Professor Rees' comments at the Toda-inspired conference, "Dialogue Among Civilizations," Okinawa, Japan, February 13, 2000.

7. Arnold J. Toynbee, *Experiences* (London: Oxford University Press, 1969), p. 83.

8. Translated from Japanese. Tsunesaburo Makiguchi, *Makiguchi Tsunesaburo zenshu* (The Complete Works of Tsunesaburo Makiguchi) (Tokyo: Daisanbunmei-sha, 1981–97), vol. 10, p. 29.

9. Ibid., p. 156.

10. Harold Pinter, 2005 Nobel Lecture: "Art, Truth & Politics," http://www.nobelprize.org/nobel_prizes/literature/laureates/2005/pinter-lecture-e.html.

## Conversation Two
## Living Up to Our Mission

1. William Shakespeare, *The Plays and Sonnets of William Shakespeare* (London: Encyclopedia Britannica, Inc., 1952), vol. 1, p. 85.

2. Ralph Waldo Emerson, *Prose Works of Ralph Waldo Emerson* (Boston: Houghton, Mifflin and Company, 1880), vol. 3, p. 220.

3. Ibid., p. 226.

4. The Soka school system, founded by Daisaku Ikeda in 1968, is based on Soka education. The Soka Junior and Senior High Schools— established by President Ikeda in Kodaira, Tokyo—were the first institutions to be established. The system now includes kindergartens, elementary, junior and senior high schools, a university in Hachioji, Tokyo, and a university in Aliso Viejo, Calif. Kindergartens

have been established in Hong Kong, Singapore, Malaysia, South Korea, and Brazil.

5. Translated from Japanese. Tsunesaburo Makiguchi, *Makiguchi Tsunesaburo zenshu* (The Complete Works of Tsunesaburo Makiguchi) (Tokyo: Daisanbunmei-sha, 1981–97), vol. 5, p. 129.

6. Ibid., p. 131.

7. *Shirokane*, ed. Shirokane Elementary School Parents Association (Tokyo: Shirokane Elementary School, 1923–31), vol. 6, pp. 18–19.

8. Bertolt Brecht, "Bread of the People," *Poems 1913–1956* (London: Methuen, 2000), p. 453.

9. Nichiren, *The Writings of Nichiren Daishonin*, vol. 2 (Tokyo: Soka Gakkai, 2006), p. 1060.

10. Translated from Japanese. Josei Toda, *Toda Josei zenshu* (The Complete Works of Josei Toda) (Tokyo: Seikyo Shimbunsha, 1981–90), vol. 4, p. 378.

11. See Richard M. Titmuss, *The Gift Relationship: From Human Blood to Social Policy* (London: New Press, 1970).

12. Saul D. Alinsky, *Reveille for Radicals* (New York: Vintage Books, 1989), p. 199.

13. Ibid., p. 174.

14. Ibid., p. 175.

15. Toda used his own funds to publish *The System of Value-Creating Pedagogy*, in which Makiguchi sets forth his student-centered pedagogic principles. When the decision to publish was made, Makiguchi described the purpose of education as "value creation," or *soka*—thus the book's title (*Soka kyoikugaku taikei* in Japanese). The book's publication, on November 18, 1930, marks the start of Soka education and the Soka Gakkai organization, originally known as the Soka Kyoiku Gakkai (Value-Creating Education Society).

16. Translated from Japanese. Tsunesaburo Makiguchi, *Makiguchi Tsunesaburo zenshu* (The Complete Works of Tsunesaburo Makiguchi) (Tokyo: Daisanbunmei-sha, 1981–97), vol. 6, p. 69.

CONVERSATION THREE
SPIRITUAL STRUGGLE

1. Daisaku Ikeda, *The Human Revolution*, book 2 (Santa Monica, Calif.: World Tribune Press, 2004), p. 1676.

2. When the north wind and the sun have a competition in the story to see who can make a traveler remove his cloak first, the sun naturally wins.

3. Judith Wright, "The Flame Tree," *Collected Poems* (Sydney: Angus & Robertson, 1994), p. 9.

4. Ibid., "Child and Wattle-tree," p. 31.

5. Ibid., "The Pool and the Star," p. 92.

## Conversation Four
## Identity And Globalization

1. The White Australia policy refers to a group of governmental policies that sought to bar people of non-European descent, particularly from Asia and the Pacific, from immigrating to Australia. The policies were eradicated between 1949 and 1973.

2. Translated from Japanese. Inazo Nitobe, *Tozai aifurete* (At the Crossroads of East and West), *Nitobe Inazo zenshu* (The Complete Works of Inazo Nitobe) (Tokyo: Kyobunkan, 1969–2001), vol. 1, p. 150.

3. Nelson Mandela, "Lighting Your Way to a Better Future," speech delivered at the launch of the Mindset Network, July 16, 2003, http://db.nelsonmandela.org/speeches/pub_view.asp?pg=item&ItemID=NMS909&txtstr=.

4. Translated from Japanese. Daisaku Ikeda, *Shishu: Jinsei no tabi* (Collected Poems: Journey of Life) (Tokyo: Seikyo Shimbunsha, 2003), pp. 286–87.

5. Translated from Japanese. *Soseki Natsume, Soseki bunmei ronshu* (Collected Essays on Civilization by Soseki Natsume), ed. Yukio Miyoshi (Tokyo: Iwanamishoten, 1986), p. 232.

## Conversation Five
## A Law for Life

1. On July 22, 2011, a lone gunman committed a series of terrorist attacks on government and civilian targets. The first, a car bomb set off in Oslo's administrative center, killed eight people, while in the second, less than two hours later, sixty-nine young people were murdered at a summer camp on the island of Utøya organized by the Workers' Youth League (AUF) of the ruling Norwegian Labour Party.

2. Save the Children, "Champions for Children: State of the World's Mothers 2011," p. 5., http://www.savethechildren.org/atf/cf/%7B9 def2ebe-10ae-432c-9bd0-df91d2eba74a%7D/SOWM2011_FULL _REPORT.PDF.

3. Ibid., p. 31.

4. Elise Boulding and Daisaku Ikeda, *Into Full Flower: Making Peace Cultures Happen* (Cambridge, Massachusetts: Dialogue Path Press, 2010), p. 20.

5. Jonas Gahr Støre, speech at the launch of the exhibition "From a Culture of Violence to a Culture of Peace: Transforming the Human Spirit" in Oslo, April 15, 2009, http://www.regjeringen.no/en/dep/ud /aktuelt/taler_artikler/utenriksministeren/2009/exhibition_open ing.html?id=555093.

6. Nichiren, *The Writings of Nichiren Daishonin*, vol. 1 (Tokyo: Soka Gakkai, 1999), p. 319.

7. Ibid., p. 656.

8. William Robertson, *Life and Times of the Right Hon. John Bright* (London: Cassell & Co., Ltd., 1889), p. 522.

9. See Nichiren, *The Writings of Nichiren Daishonin*, vol. 2, p. 931.

10. Daisaku Ikeda, *A Lasting Peace: Collected Addresses of Daisaku Ikeda* (New York: Weatherhill Inc., 1981), vol. 1, p. 218.

11. "Human revolution" is the SGI concept that self-motivated, positive change within the individual will bring about a change in the individual's immediate environment—a process that will ultimately effect a change in society.

12. André Maurois, *Au commencement était l'action* (In the Beginning Was Action) (Paris: Librairie Plon, 1966), p. 93.

CONVERSATION SIX
UNSUNG HEROES

1. Nichiren, *The Writings of Nichiren Daishonin*, vol. 1, p. 457.

2. Translated from Japanese. Tsunesaburo Makiguchi, *Makiguchi Tsunesaburo zenshu* (The Complete Works of Tsunesaburo Makiguchi) (Tokyo: Daisanbunmei-sha, 1981–97), vol. 8, p. 49.

3. See http://www.newsweek.com/25-most-desirable-small-schools -71881 and http://www.newsweek.com/25-most-diverse-schools -71887. Both posted to the Newsweek website, September 12, 2010.

4. Vincent Harding and Daisaku Ikeda, *America Will Be!: Conversations on Hope, Freedom, and Democracy* (Cambridge, Massachusetts: Dialogue Path Press, 2013), p. 95.

5. Ibid., p. 97.

6. Ralph Waldo Emerson, *The Journals and Miscellaneous Notebooks of Ralph Waldo Emerson*, ed. Alfred R. Ferguson et al. (Boston: Harvard University Press, 1960–82), vol. 4, pp. 353–54.

7. Translated from Japanese. Daisaku Ikeda, *Wasureenu deai* (Unforgettable Encounters) (Tokyo: Seikyo Shimbunsha, 1982), p. 152.

8. In Daisaku Ikeda, "Our Struggles Are Our Treasures" (October 10, 2014, *World Tribune*), p. 4.

9. These lyrics are from "Song of Human Revolution" (Feb. 12, 2016, *World Tribune*), p. 1.

10. Daisaku Ikeda, "Toward a World of Dignity for All," 2011 peace proposal.

Conversation Seven
A World Without Nuclear Weapons

1. Translated from Japanese. Nobu Shirase, *Nankyoku tanken* (The Antarctic Expedition) (Tokyo: Chikuma Shobo, 1962), p. 22.

2. Ibid., p. 116.

3. See Ibid., pp. 114–15.

4. Translated from Japanese. Cho Moon-Boo and Daisaku Ikeda, *Kibo no seiki e takara no kakehashi* (The Bridge toward a Century of Hope) (Tokyo: Tokuma Shoten, 2002), p. 26.

5. See Chang Jen-Hu and Daisaku Ikeda, *Ningenshori no shunju rekishi to jinsei to kyoiku o kataru* (An Epoch of Human Triumph: A Dialogue on History, Life and Education) (Tokyo: Daisanbunmei-sha, 2010), p. 44.

6. In 1861, in a bay in the area of Western Australia now known as Broome, divers discovered the *Pinctada maxima* oyster, which possessed the largest pearl shell in the world. The material of the inner shell, called "Mother of Pearl," quickly became the primary material for the production of buttons worldwide. Over the coming decades, experienced divers came to Broome from all over East and Southeast Asia to work, joining the local Aboriginals. The female Japanese

divers, known as the "Ama," were considered the best of all divers at this challenging task. The divers worked under often-horrible conditions, for little pay. Today in Broome, the Japanese cemetery features more than 900 engraved gravestones commemorating the divers who lost their lives performing this work.

7. Translated from Japanese. Tsunesaburo Makiguchi, *Makiguchi Tsunesaburo zenshu* (The Complete Works of Tsunesaburo Makiguchi) (Tokyo: Daisanbunmei-sha, 1981–97), vol. 1, p. 13.

8. Oodgeroo Noonuccal, "All One Race," *My People: A Kath Walker Collection* (Milton: The Jacaranda Press, 1981), p. 1.

9. Joseph Rotblat and Daisaku Ikeda, *A Quest for Global Peace: Rotblat and Ikeda on War, Ethics and the Nuclear Threat* (London: I.B. Tauris, 2007), p. 116.

10. Ibid., p. 122.

11. Daisaku Ikeda, "The Evil Over Which We Must Triumph," *From the Ashes: A Spiritual Response to the Attack on America* (Emmaus, Pennsylvania: Rodale Inc. and Beliefnet, Inc., 2001), p. 106.

12. The Review Conference of the Parties to the Treaty on the Non-Proliferation of Nuclear Weapons was held at the United Nations in New York from April 27 to May 22, 2015.

13. Daisaku Ikeda, "Toward a World of Dignity for All: The Triumph of the Creative Life," 2011 peace proposal, http://www.daisakuikeda. org/assets/files/peace2011.pdf.

14. Established by Stuart Rees in 1998 and awarded by the Sydney Peace Foundation, the Sydney Peace Prize honors individuals who have exhibited leadership in areas including human rights, social justice, human rights, and nonviolent conflict resolution. The goal is to raise awareness and stimulate interest in peacebuilding among the general public.

15. Ikeda, "Toward a World of Dignity for All," 2011 peace proposal.

16. The conference on a Weapon-of-Mass-Destruction-Free Zone (WMDFZ) in the Middle East cited in the final document of the Non-Proliferation Treaty (NPT) Review Conference in 2010, which was supposed to be held in 2012, was ultimately postponed by the three Signatory States: Russia, the United Kingdom, and the United States.

17. Shirase, *Nankyoku tanken* (The Antarctic Expedition), p. 29.

CONVERSATION EIGHT
CREATING THE CONDITIONS FOR PEACE

1. See Josef Derbolav and Daisaku Ikeda, *Search for a New Humanity* (New York: Weatherhill, 1992), p. 238.

2. See Johan Galtung and Daisaku Ikeda, *Choose Peace* (London: Pluto Press, 1995), p. 7.

3. Benedict de Spinoza, *The Chief Works of Benedict de Spinoza*, trans. R. H. M. Elwes (London: George Bell and Sons, 1883), vol. 1, p. 314.

4. Victor Hugo, *Poems* (Rockville, Maryland: Wildside Press LLC, 2009), pp. 273–74.

5. Desmond Tutu, *No Future without Forgiveness* (London: Random House, 1999), pp. 34–35.

6. *The Sutta-Nipata*, trans. H. Saddhatissa (London: Curzon Press, 1994), verses 148 and 149, p. 16.

7. Ibid., verse 936, p. 17.

8. Ibid., verses 704 and 705, pp. 81–82.

9. Elise Boulding and Randall Forsberg, *Abolishing War* (Cambridge, Mass.: Boston Research Center for the 21st Century, 1998), p. 40.

10. John Burton, "A Regional Strategy: From Strategic Deterrence to Problem Solving," *Essays on Peace*, eds. Michael Sala, Walter Tonetto and Earlque Martinez (Queensland: Central Queensland University Press, 1995), pp. 143–44.

11. United Nations Development Programme, "Human Development Report 2004," p. 43, http://hdr.undp.org/sites/default/files/reports/265/hdr_2004_complete.pdf.

12. M. E. David, *Professor David: The Life of Sir Edgeworth David* (London: Edward Arnold & Co., 1937), p. 38.

13. Tsunesaburo Makiguchi, Josei Toda, and Daisaku Ikeda.

14. See https://www.soka.ac.jp/en/about/philosophy/mission/.

15. Oscar Arias Sánchez, *Horizons of Peace: the Costa Rican Contribution to the Peace Process in Central America* (San José: Arias Foundation for Peace and Human Progress, 1994), p. 86.

16. Jorge Debravo, *Nosotros, los hombres* (We, Mankind) (San José: Editorial Costa Rica, 1994), pp. 61–62.

## CONVERSATION NINE
## POETRY TO REAWAKEN

1. Percy Bysshe Shelley, "A Defence of Poetry," *English Essays: From Sir Philip Sidney to Macaulay*; with Introduction and notes, ed. Charles W. Eliot, LL.D. (New York: P.F. Collier and Son, 1909), vol. 27, p. 360.
2. Percy Bysshe Shelley, *An Address to the Irish People*, eds. Thomas William Rolleston and Thomas James Wise (London: Reeves and Turner, 1890), p. 12.
3. Shelley, "A Defence of Poetry," p. 377.
4. Harding and Ikeda, *America Will Be!*, p. 209.
5. Toynbee, *Experiences*, p. 313.
6. Ibid., pp. 320–21.
7. Daisaku Ikeda, "Passion Is the Proof" (Nov. 12, 1999, *World Tribune*), p. 4.
8. Shelley, "A Defence of Poetry," p. 354.
9. Simone Weil, *The Need for Roots: Prelude to a Declaration of Duties Towards Mankind*, trans. A. F. Willis (London and New York: Routledge, 2001), p. 172.
10. John Donne, *The Works of John Donne*, ed. Henry Alford (London: John W. Parker, 1939), vol. 3, p. 575.
11. Nichiren, *Writings*, vol. 1, p. 852.
12. Percy Bysshe Shelley, "Proposals for an Association of Philanthropists," *The Prose Works of Percy Bysshe Shelley*, ed. Richard Herne Shepherd (London: Chatto and Windus, 1810), p. 269.
13. *The Record of the Orally Transmitted Teachings* (Tokyo: Soka Gakkai, 2004), p. 146.
14. Noonuccal, "A Song of Hope," *My People*, p. 40.
15. Percy Bysshe Shelley, *The Masque of Anarchy: A Poem* (London: Edward Moxon, 1832), p. 20.

## CONVERSATION TEN
## FIGHTING FOR WHAT IS RIGHT

1. Jessie Street, *Jessie Street: A Revised Autobiography*, ed. Lenore Coltheart (Sydney: The Federation Press, 2004), p. 161.
2. Mahatma Gandhi, *My Non-violence* (Ahmedabad: Navajivan Pub. House, 1960), p. 36.

3. Translated from Japanese. Daisaku Ikeda, *Watakushi no sekai koy-uroku* (Intimate Talks with Global Pioneers), *Ikeda Daisaku zenshu* (The Complete Works of Daisaku Ikeda), vol. 122 (Tokyo: Seikyo Shimbun-sha, 2002), p. 347.

4. Ibid., p. 353.

5. Harper Lee, *To Kill a Mockingbird* (New York: Warner Books, 1982), p. 88.

6. Ibid., pp. 104–05.

7. Clarence Darrow, *Attorney for the Damned: Clarence Darrow in the Courtroom*, ed. Arthur Weinberg (Chicago: University of Chicago Press, 1989).

8. In 1956, the Soka Gakkai for the first time fielded candidates in the House of Councillors (Upper House) national election in Japan. Ultimately, three candidates were elected, including a candidate running in the Osaka district in a campaign led by Ikeda. A number of Soka Gakkai members were subsequently charged with violating aspects of the Election Law, and prosecutors tried to hold Ikeda responsible. In July 1957, Ikeda was arrested and detained for two weeks; in the subsequent trial, however, he was completely exonerated. The case was one of the first post-war examples of harassment of the Soka Gakkai caused by its rising political influence.

9. Daisaku Ikeda, *The Human Revolution*, book 2 (Santa Monica, Calif.: World Tribune Press, 2001), pp. 1682–83.

10. Translated from Japanese. Makiguchi, *Zenshu*, vol. 10, p. 26.

11. Edward W. Saïd, *Representations of the Intellectual: The 1993 Reith Lectures* (London: Vintage, 1994), p. 31.

12. Marianne Moore, ed. and intr. Patricia C. Willis, *The Complete Prose of Marianne Moore* (New York: Viking, 1986), p. 513.

13. David Krieger and Daisaku Ikeda, *Choose Hope: Your Role in Waging Peace in the Nuclear Age* (Santa Monica, Calif.: Middleway Press, 2002), pp. 64–65.

14. Hannah Arendt, *Men in Dark Times* (New York: Harcourt, Brace & World, 1968), p. 22.

15. The seven parables that appear in the Lotus Sutra include: 1) the parable of the three carts and the burning house, 2) the parable of the wealthy man and his poor son, 3) the parable of the three kinds of medicinal herbs and two kinds of trees, 4) the parable of the phantom city and the treasure land, 5) the parable of the jewel in the robe,

6) the parable of the bright jewel in the topknot, and 7) the parable of the skilled physician and his sick children.

16. See the "Simile and Parable" (third) chapter of *The Lotus Sutra and Its Opening and Closing Sutras*, trans. Burton Watson (Tokyo: Soka Gakkai, 2009), pp. 82–116.

17. *The Lotus Sutra and Its Opening and Closing Sutras*, p. 128.

18. See the "Belief and Understanding" (fourth) chapter of *The Lotus Sutra and Its Opening and Closing Sutras*, pp. 117–133.

19. *The Lotus Sutra and Its Opening and Closing Sutras*, p. 124.

20. Marianne Moore, *Complete Poems* (New York: Penguin Books, 1994), p. 95.

21. Ikeda, *Shishu: Jinsei no tabi*, p. 124.

CONVERSATION ELEVEN
DIGNITY FOR ALL

1. Translated from Japanese. Toda, *zenshu*, vol. 4, p. 529.

2. Daisaku Ikeda, "Toward a New Era of Value Creation," 2010 peace proposal.

3. CNN, August 15, 2011, "World Bank Chief: Global Economy In 'New Danger Zone'," http://edition.cnn.com/2011/BUSINESS/08/14/world.bank.danger/index.html.

4. See *The Financial Times* (London), August 14, 2011, "The Dangers of Youth's Labour Lost" http://www.ft.com/intl/cms/s/0/d60obbc9c-c4dc-11e0-9c4d-00144feabdco.html#axzz1mzpnqlxY.

5. Stuart Rees, Gordon Rodley, and Frank Stilwell, *Beyond the Market: Alternatives to Economic Rationalism* (Leichhardt: Pluto Press Australia, 1993), p. 222.

6. Franklin D. Roosevelt, *The Public Papers and Addresses of Franklin D. Roosevelt* (New York: Random House, 1933), vol. 2, p. 271.

7. John Kenneth Galbraith, *The Affluent Society, Fortieth Anniversary Edition* (New York: Houghton Mifflin Company, 1998), p. 191.

8. On September 17, 2011, protesters occupied Zuccotti Park in the Wall Street financial district of New York City, where they stayed until they were forced out on November 15. With their slogan of "We are the 99 percent," they sought to draw attention to income inequality and unjust wealth distribution in the United States and in the financial systems they see as biased in favor of

large corporations, the financial services sector, and the already wealthy, all of whom are identified as the "1 percent." They sought to make decisions through decentralized, participatory processes. Their action inspired similar occupation protests across the United States.

9. Translated from Japanese. Josei Toda, *Toda Josei zenshu* (The Complete Works of Josei Toda) (Tokyo: Seikyo Shimbun-sha, 1984), vol. 1, p. 28.

10. Aristotle, *The Nicomachean Ethics* (Bk. I: Ch. 6), trans. David Ross (New York: Oxford University Press, 2009), p. 7.

11. See Daisaku Ikeda, "Toward Humanitarian Competition," 2009 peace proposal, in *A Forum for Peace*, pp. 311–342.

12. Daisaku Ikeda, "Humanizing Religion, Creating Peace," 2008 peace proposal, http://www.daisakuikeda.org/assets/files/pp2008.pdf.

## CONVERSATION TWELVE
## ALTRUSIM OVER EGOISM

1. UNFPA (United Nations Population Fund), "World Population to Reach 7 Billion on 31 October," UNFPA News, May 3, 2011, http://un.by/unfpa/en/news/world/26u.html.

2. UNFPA, "The State of World Population 2011: People and Possibilities in a World of 7 Billion," p. 121, http://foweb.unfpa.org/SWP2011/reports/EN-SWOP2011-FINAL.pdf.

3. Muhammad Yunus and Alan Jolis, *Banker to the Poor: The Autobiography of Muhammad Yunus, Founder of Grameen Bank* (Dhaka: The University Press Ltd., 1998), p. 82.

4. Muhammad Yunus and Karl Weber, *Creating a World without Poverty: Social Business and the Future of Capitalism* (New York: Public Affairs, 2007), p. 239.

5. Olara A. Otunnu, former Ambassador of Uganda to the United Nations (1980–85), UN Under-Secretary-General, and Special Representative for Children and Armed Conflict (1998–2005).

6. Hans Blix, former Director General of the International Atomic Energy Agency (1981–97) and Chair of the Weapons of Mass Destruction Commission (2003–09).

7. H. V. Evatt, *Australia in World Affairs* (Sydney: Angus and Robertson, 1946), pp. 25–26.

8. Yunus and Jolis, *Banker to the Poor*, p. 78.

9. Ibid., p. 230.

10. Yunus and Weber, *Creating a World Without Poverty*, p. 55.

11. Street, *Jessie Street: A Revised Autobiography*, p. 213.

12. Daisaku Ikeda's speech at the Youth Division March 16 Commemorative Meeting held at the Soka International Friendship Hall in Sendagaya, Tokyo, on March 13, 1998.

13. Tsunesaburo Makiguchi, *A Geography of Human Life*, trans. Dayle M. Bethel (San Francisco: Caddo Gap Press, 2002), p. 284.

14. William Wordsworth, "Humanity," *The Poetical Works of William Wordsworth* (London: Edward Moxon, 1837), vol. v, p. 109.

15. Yunus and Jolis, *Banker to the Poor*, p. 4.

16. Ibid.

17. Ibid., p. 140.

18. Aurelio Peccei and Daisaku Ikeda, *Before It Is Too Late* (London: I.B. Tauris, 2009), p. 110.

19. Judith Wright, *With Love and Fury: Selected Letters*, ed. Patricia Clarke and Meredith McKinney (Queensland: University of Queensland Press, 2004), p. 34.

20. Mary Cameron Gilmore, *The Collected Verse of Mary Gilmore: 1887–1929*, ed. Jennifer Strauss (Queensland: University of Queensland Press, 2006), vol. 1, p. 161.

# Index

against poor people, 173–74
racial, 31, 94, 130, 133, 141–42
diversity, 35, 71, 145. *See also*
multiculturalism
Doherty, Denis, 84
Donne, John, 130

economic crisis, 155–59, 176
mechanisms for preventing, 178
resolution of, 176–77
economics, 161–63. *See also*
economic crisis
ethical principles and, 163–64
humanitarian competition and,
176–77, 179
human rights and, 178–79
real-life, 172–83
social systems and, 165
social values and, 165
economic theories, impotence of,
179
education, xix, 22–25, 52–53, 77–78,
80, 125, 159, 180, 190n4. *See also*
*specific schools*
of children, 140–41, 174
correspondence education, 54–56
empathy and, 128–29
of girls and women, 174
humanistic, 24, 77–78, 136
human rights and, 137–40, 145–47
passion and, 126–28
self-teaching, 79–80
student-centered learning, 117
as value-creation, 191n15
value of, 71–72
efficiency, 160–64
egoism, xix, 26, 29, 166, 169–84
Egypt, 52, 89
Emerson, Ralph Waldo, 21–22,
84–85
empathy, 136
compassionate, 131–36
education and, 128–29
social issues and, 128–29
employment, dignity and, 155–59
empowerment, 181
"Engaging the Other" core research
program, Toda Institute for
Global Peace and Policy
Research, 109
environmental destruction, 2

environmental protection, xix, 46,
178
"Eternal Treasures of Japan"
exhibition, 58–59
ethical principles, economics and,
163–64
Europe
civil society in, 170
economic crisis and, 157
market-based society in, 170
Evatt, H. V., 171
exploitation, 165, 166

families, as children's first school,
140–41
famine, 166, 179
fascism, 32, 110
fatalism, overcoming, 156, 180
Festival of Health, Kansai Soka
schools, 23
Fischer, Louis, *The Life of Mahatma
Gandhi*, 148
food-supply crisis, 2
foolishness, 166, 178
foreign policy, 126
freedom
development and, 164–65
interpretations of, 178
free market economics, 160–61, 163,
170, 176
Friends of the CTBT, 98
Fukushima Nuclear Power Plant, 39

Galbraith, John Kenneth, 159–61,
164
Galtung, Johan, 63, 108–9, 130
Gandhi, Arun, 69–70, 72–73
Gandhi, Mahatma, xix, 38, 61, 71–72,
90, 115, 124, 139, 148–49
Gandhi, Manilal, 69–70
Gandhi, Sushila, 69
Gaviria Trujillo, César, 60
gender-based discrimination, 86,
108, 172–74
generosity, 27
Germany, in World War II, 110
gift relationship, 26–34, 176
Gillard, Julia, 47–48
Gilmore, Mary, 182
girls, education of, 174
global citizenship, 5

# About the Authors

STUART REES is professor emeritus at the University of Sydney and former director of the Sydney Peace Foundation. Born in England, he was the founding director of Sydney's Centre for Peace and Conflict Studies and served in that position for eighteen years. He is a former member of the University of Sydney Senate and of the NSW Government's Reconciliation Commission. He is also the independent chair of the State's Energy Council and an administrator of the international project to create a UN Emergency Peace Service. In 2005, he received the Order of Australia for services to international relations. Rees's career has included social work positions in Britain and Canada and community development responsibilities in India, Sri Lanka, and in the War on Poverty programs in the United States. He has taught at major universities in the UK and North America and was previously professor of social work at the University of Sydney. His publications include over one hundred journal articles on topics such as evaluations of health and welfare services, the attributes of peace negotiations, and humanitarianism in social policy. He is the author and coauthor of ten books, including *Beyond the Market; Human Rights, Corporate Responsibility; Passion for Peace: Exercising Power Creatively*, and the poetry anthology, *Tell Me the Truth About War.*

DAISAKU IKEDA is president of the Soka Gakkai International, a lay Buddhist organization with more than twelve million members worldwide. He has written and lectured widely on Buddhism, humanism, and global ethics. More than fifty of his dialogues have been published, including *Choose Life* with Arnold J. Toynbee, *Moral Lessons of the Twentieth Century* with Mikhail Gorbachev, *A*

*Quest for Global Peace* with Joseph Rotblat, *New Horizons in Eastern Humanism* with Tu Weiming, and *America Will Be!: Conversations on Hope, Freedom, and Democracy* with Vincent Harding. Dedicated to education that promotes humanistic ideals, Mr. Ikeda founded Soka University in Tokyo in 1971 and, in 2001, Soka University of America in Aliso Viejo, California. In furtherance of his vision of fostering dialogue and solidarity for peace, Mr. Ikeda has founded three independent, nonprofit research institutes: the Ikeda Center for Peace, Learning, and Dialogue, the Toda Institute for Global Peace and Policy Research, and the Institute of Oriental Philosophy. He has received many academic honors, including the United Nations Peace Award in 1983.

# Titles from Dialogue Path Press
All titles coauthored by Daisaku Ikeda

SHAPING A NEW SOCIETY: CONVERSATIONS ON ECONOMICS, EDUCATION, AND PEACE (2017) *Envisioning healthy societies, in Asia and globally.* With Lawrence J. Lau, former Professor of Economics, Stanford University, and former Vice-Chancellor, Chinese University of Hong Kong

KNOWING OUR WORTH: CONVERSATIONS ON ENERGY AND SUSTAINABILITY (2016) *On healing the planet and moving toward an environmentally sustainable future.* With Ernst Ulrich von Weizsäcker, former Dean, Donald Bren School of Environmental Science and Management, University of California, Santa Barbara, and co-president of the Club of Rome

OUR WORLD TO MAKE: HINDUISM, BUDDHISM, AND THE RISE OF GLOBAL CIVIL SOCIETY (2015) *Presenting a vision for the future of a global civil society based on our shared humanity.* With Ved Nanda, Evans University Professor and Thompson G. Marsh Professor of Law, University of Denver

LIVING AS LEARNING: JOHN DEWEY IN THE 21ST CENTURY (2014) *Exploring the contemporary, cross-cultural relevance of John Dewey's philosophy of education.* With Jim Garrison, Professor of Philosophy of Education, Virginia Tech University and Larry A. Hickman, Director, Center for Dewey Studies, and Professor of Philosophy, Southern Illinois University Carbondale

THE ART OF TRUE RELATIONS: CONVERSATIONS ON THE POETIC HEART OF HUMAN POSSIBILITY (2014) *Illuminating the bonds that form the foundation of the human experience.* With Sarah Wider, Professor of English and Women's Studies, Colgate University

AMERICA WILL BE!: CONVERSATIONS ON HOPE, FREEDOM, AND DEMOCRACY (2013) *Insightful perspectives on the unfolding of the American civil rights movement.* With Vincent Harding, author and confidant of Martin Luther King Jr., and chairperson of the Veterans of Hope Project, Iliff School of Theology

THE INNER PHILOSOPHER: CONVERSATIONS ON PHILOSOPHY'S TRANSFORMATIVE POWER (2012) *An empowering look at the wisdom and practical application of philosophy.* With Lou Marinoff, Professor and Chair of Philosophy, The City College of New York

INTO FULL FLOWER: MAKING PEACE CULTURES HAPPEN (2010) *Two peace activists shed light on the process of peace building.* With Elise M. Boulding, Professor of Sociology Emerita, Dartmouth College

CREATING WALDENS: AN EAST-WEST CONVERSATION ON THE AMERICAN RENAISSANCE (2009) *An exploration of the spiritual and ethical insights of Emerson, Thoreau, and Whitman.* With Ronald A. Bosco, Distinguished Professor of English and American Literature, University at Albany, State University of New York and Joel Myerson, Carolina Distinguished Professor of American Literature, Emeritus, University of South Carolina